The Use of U.S. Power

The **Institute for the Study of Diplomacy** (ISD), founded in 1978, is a program of Georgetown University's Edmund A. Walsh School of Foreign Service and is the School's primary window on the world of the foreign affairs practitioner.

ISD studies the practitioner's craft: how diplomats and other foreign affairs professionals succeed and the lessons to be learned from their successes and failures. Institute programs focus on the foreign policy process: how decisions are made and implemented.

ISD conducts its programs through a small staff and resident and nonresident "associates." Associates, primarily U.S. and foreign government officials, are detailed to or affiliated with the Institute for a year or more. The Institute seeks to build academic-practitioner collaborations around issues using associates and Georgetown faculty. ISD staff and associates teach courses, organize lectures and discussions, mentor students, and participate on university committees.

In addition, ISD's Pew Case Studies in International Affairs are used in over 1,000 courses across the country and around the world.

The
Use *of*
U.S. Power

Implications for U.S. Interests

STANLEY R. SLOAN

ROBERT G. SUTTER

CASIMIR A. YOST

Institute for the Study of Diplomacy
Edmund A. Walsh School of Foreign Service
GEORGETOWN UNIVERSITY

Institute for the Study of Diplomacy
Edmund A. Walsh School of Foreign Service
Georgetown University, Washington, D.C. 20057–1025
© 2004 by the Institute for the Study of Diplomacy.

ISBN 0-934742-97-9
Printed in the United States of America

Contents

Preface

At the opening of the twenty-first century, the United States stood alone as the one truly global power. That position carried with it opportunities and responsibilities of a new order of magnitude.

The September 11 terrorist attacks produced profound sympathy and offers of assistance from around the world and particularly from our allies and partners in Europe and Asia. The United States, however, failed to build on the strong foundation offered by the wave of post-9/11 international support. International divisions have cut into U.S. influence around the globe. U.S. power remains unmatched, but the ability of the United States to meet its objectives in the war on terrorism, in the Middle East, and with its key allies has eroded.

Against this backdrop, the Institute for the Study of Diplomacy at the Edmund A. Walsh School of Foreign Service at Georgetown University initiated a project in mid-2003 to examine the consequences of this series of developments for U.S. interests. The institute's director, Casimir A. Yost, Georgetown Professor Robert G. Sutter, and Stanley R. Sloan, visiting scholar at Middlebury College and director of the Atlantic Community Initiative, undertook to analyze the issue from the perspective of U.S. foreign policy challenges and the consequences of European and Asian responses to the use of U.S. power.

The project initially produced three papers: "U.S. Power and Influence in the Middle East and South Asia," "U.S. Power and Influence in Europe," and "U.S. Power and Influence in Asia," the core chapters of this monograph. The latter two papers were presented on a panel at the annual meeting of the International Studies Association in Montreal, Canada, on March 18, 2004.

On April 26, 2004, the Schlesinger Working Group on Strategic Surprises convened at Georgetown University to critique the three drafts and to speculate on developments that could challenge both conventional wisdom and U.S. policies. The discussion, led by Chester A. Crocker of Georgetown University and the United States Institute of Peace, yielded a wide variety of helpful perspectives and constructive criticisms, which the study authors acknowledge with gratitude. The session also produced a range of views on "strategic surprises," which are captured in the working group's meeting summary, published as an appendix to this monograph.

The project leaders next wrote an overview chapter entitled "The Future Stewardship of American Power," which opens the Institute's monograph. The three specific regional chapters follow. All have benefited from the review and input provided during the spring by the Schlesinger Working Group and individual reviewers.

The release of this analysis could not be more timely. The United States is turning over political control of Iraq to the Iraqis, but the challenge of shepherding the country toward a stable and productive future is far from finished. There is a growing debate in the United States, which cuts across party lines, about what goals are legitimate and attainable in Iraq and in the broader Middle East. The United Nations is once again an active participant in efforts to put Iraq on a positive course. North American Treaty Organization (NATO) allies are attempting to rebuild a degree of mutual trust and unity that has been severely damaged by differences over Iraq. And the United States is in the midst of a political campaign that will determine the leadership of the next U.S. administration. Whether the outcome is a second term for George W. Bush, or a new administration led by the Democratic Party's presumptive nominee Senator John Kerry, the administration will have to try to begin restoring respect for and faith in the United States around the globe.

Events of the past few years have demonstrated that modern security challenges, including those growing out of radical Islamic movements such as Al-Qaeda, must be met with a variety of policy instruments. Diplomacy, economic policies, support from allies, and the legitimizing involvement of international organizations, particularly the United Nations, need to be deployed alongside military force. Such a spectrum of approaches is required to diminish the root causes of terrorism, control the proliferation of weapons of mass destruction, and mitigate instability caused by failed or rogue states.

In today's world, there undoubtedly will be occasions when the United States is forced to act alone to defend its vital interests. Long-term U.S. interests, however, depend on gaining international support and legitimacy for America's foreign policy.

The Institute for the Study of Diplomacy and the authors appreciate the grant provided by the Carnegie Corporation of New York, which made this project possible. Of course, the statements made and views expressed in this monograph are solely the responsibility of the three authors.

Thomas R. Pickering
Chairman

L. Thomas Hiltz   Peter F. Krogh
Vice Chairmen
Board of Directors
Institute for the Study of Diplomacy

Introduction

Since the September 11, 2001, terrorist attacks on targets in New York and Washington, the United States has faced unprecedented challenges to protect itself from further attacks while seeking to eliminate the sources of terror abroad. The way in which U.S. power has been used since 9/11 has proven to be a source of division both at home and abroad. In particular, the war against Iraq, although successful in removing Saddam Hussein from power, has alienated the United States from key allies and has undermined the image and influence of the United States throughout the world. This in turn has affected the U.S. ability to protect and advance U.S. interests internationally.

This study examines the way the United States has deployed its power resources since 9/11 and assesses the impact of U.S. decisions on the problems of terrorism, the Israeli-Palestinian struggle, Middle East instability, and the proliferation of weapons of mass destruction. It then focuses on how U.S. policy has affected the U.S.'s ability to influence the policies and behaviors of key allies and partners in Europe and Asia. The study's conclusions focus on the consequences of this interaction for U.S. interests.

Drawing on the detailed analyses that follow in subsequent chapters, the monograph's first chapter summarizes the authors' judgments concerning how effectively the United States has used its power to meet the post-9/11 international challenges. The monograph's main goal is to suggest how the next U.S. administration, taking office in January 2005, could repair some of the damage done, particularly by the war in Iraq, and pursue directions more likely to produce favorable outcomes for U.S. interests in the Middle East and in relations with key allies and partners in Europe and Asia.

1

1

The Future Stewardship
of American Power:
Conclusions and Recommendations

The United States is uniquely powerful. U.S. military capabilities are unmatched. Moreover, the United States has demonstrated a willingness to utilize its military power in pursuit of its interests in Kosovo, in Afghanistan, in Iraq, and in combating terrorism. During the 1990s, there were questions about whether the United States had become "self-deterred," unwilling to use military force to achieve its objectives if casualties would be incurred. Today, no one doubts the U.S. willingness to respond militarily if challenged.

Of course, U.S. "power" is not just military. It is economic and political and cultural as well. It is multidimensional and more imposing as a result. The overwhelming fact of American power guarantees that other nations must adjust to and position themselves vis-à-vis the United States. As John Ikenberry puts it, "Governments are trying to figure out how an American-centered unipolar order will operate. How will the United States use its power? Will a unipolar world be built around rules and institutions or the unilateral exercise of American power?"[1]

The experience of other governments post-9/11 has not been reassuring. There have been growing international fears of unbridled American power. How the United States utilizes the enormous power

---

*This chapter was prepared by Stanley R. Sloan, Robert G. Sutter, and Casimir A. Yost.

at its disposal has become a critical factor in America's ability to bring other nations together behind its leadership.

Some Americans, in and out of positions of authority, have been so taken with the fact of preponderant U.S. power that they have urged that it be used to shape the international environment to its preferences and design. "The mission of the United States," writes Corey Robin, "was now clear to conservatives: to defend civilization and freedom against barbarism and terror."2 Those holding such views have tended to judge that because the United States is uniquely powerful, it can act largely on its own or with ad hoc, temporary coalitions. This proposition is being tested and found wanting in the Middle East and in relations with key U.S. allies.

The dilemma, which has become more apparent with the passage of time, is that overwhelming power does not equate to overwhelming influence—the ability to get others to act to the U.S. benefit. Achieving influence over the decisions of others all too often requires more than raw power, though power, carefully applied, can on occasion make a critical difference. Influence requires effective diplomacy, persuasive argumentation, consensus building, and appeal to interests held in common. Finding the right balance between such "soft power" resources and U.S. "hard power" capabilities is the challenge U.S. administrations face in their stewardship of U.S. power and interests.

Moreover, U.S. leaders are beginning to appreciate some of the limitations on U.S. power. U.S. dependence on imported foreign energy drives U.S. administrations to take risks that might otherwise be avoided. Prosecuting the war on terrorism requires the United States to build relationships with dictatorial and repressive regimes, giving substance to the charge that America espouses à la carte democracy. Further, the United States is discovering that with all its power U.S. administrations nonetheless face fiscal and manpower limits as deficits rise and U.S. forces are stretched dangerously thin in Iraq and around the globe.

It is fair to say that the Bush administration did not fully appreciate the enormity of the task facing it after 9/11. Presented with unprecedented challenges, the administration took a series of steps, deemed necessary and desirable at the time, that have complicated the prospects for U.S. success. A rapid, decisive attack on the Taliban and Al-Qaeda in Afghanistan was necessary. But then the administration seemed to go off track. The rhetorical devaluing of long-time allies and institutional relationships complicated the administration's ability to bring others into a cooperative approach to the Iraq problem both before and after the war. It was a measure of America's diminished influence that previously close and friendly countries like Turkey, Germany, Mexico, and Chile opposed the United States before the outbreak of the Iraq conflict and that India, France, and other countries would not assist the U.S.-led coalition with troops after the conflict.

Bush administration officials relied on the presence of WMD in Iraq to support the necessity of preemptive action and to vindicate their decision to invade Iraq. The failure to find these weapons seriously hampered U.S. efforts to mobilize international support for Iraq's political and economic reconstruction. The widespread perception was that administration critics, not the administration, had been vindicated by the unfolding of events in Iraq.

The United States entered Iraq with sufficient forces to win the war but woefully inadequate numbers to secure the peace. The coalition never really took complete control, and so the Coalition Provisional Authority was in a reactive mode from its inception, unable to shape events. The gap between America's promise of a better future for all Iraqis and the deteriorating security situation in Iraq became formidable. On May 13, 2004, the *Washington Post* reported, "Four out of five Iraqis report holding a negative view of the U.S. occupation authority and of coalition forces, according to a new poll conducted for the occupation authority."[3]

U.S. moral authority has always been a key element of U.S. soft power. Even before revelations of U.S. mistreatment of Iraqi detainees, the war in Iraq had severely diminished the U.S. claim to the high ground in this area. The Abu Ghraib prisoner scandal has had a devastating impact on the U.S. image in the Muslim world and around the globe. Such damage will not be repaired quickly or easily.

The war in Iraq, of course, has not occurred in a vacuum. Despite Bush administration denials, resources, human and financial, have been diverted from Afghanistan and the war on terrorism to prosecute the conflict in Iraq. Relationships with friends in the Middle East have been strained, with images of war parading across television screens throughout the region. And, the ripple effects of the war have been felt in Europe and Asia.

Implications in Europe

The terrorist attacks on the United States and the nature of the U.S. response had a major impact on U.S.-European relations. The 9/11 attacks left fundamentally different impressions on Americans and Europeans. Americans, led by President Bush, had adopted a "war mentality" that seemed to warrant all necessary steps to defend the country, irrespective of the views of other countries or the accepted norms of international law. Europeans, although shocked and sympathetic, did not see the attacks as changing global realities in any profound way. They remained convinced that international cooperation and law remained vitally important foundations for international stability and, indeed, for a struggle against international terrorism.

Immediately following 9/11, key officials in the Bush administration began to act on the assumption that Saddam Hussein was part of the terrorist problem that should, and could, be eliminated. While the United States was laying the groundwork for an attack against Saddam Hussein's Iraq, the European allies were not prepared to come to the same conclusions reached already by Bush administration officials. Europeans generally agreed that Hussein was a problem and that his regime was in clear violation of international law. Further, they shared some of the U.S. frustration that international sanctions had done much to hurt the Iraqi people but not enough to undermine Saddam's rule.

However, most Europeans and many European governments reacted strongly to the Bush administration's determination to go to war against Iraq no matter what other countries thought, irrespective of how unilateral action might affect the future of international cooperation, and with little regard for the impact on international law.

Although the unilateral U.S. approach to Iraq was the instigating event for the crisis in U.S.-European relations, French President Jacques Chirac and German Chancellor Gerhard Schroeder helped make it a full-blown crisis that produced deep divisions among Europeans as well as between many Europeans and the United States. Given German public opinion in the summer of 2002, Chancellor Schroeder undoubtedly needed to take a stand against attacking Iraq in order to be returned as chancellor in the fall elections. But Schroeder disappointed many Americans, and surely President Bush, by failing to soften his opposition after the election. France's criticism of the U.S. stance was seen in Washington, and across the country, as typical Gaullist grandstanding designed to show France's flag and to rein in the U.S. hegemon. As in the case of Germany, however, As in the case of Germany, however, French government opposition to the war was consistent with French public opinion.

The consequences for U.S. interests have been profound. British Prime Minister Tony Blair remained a staunch ally for U.S. policy toward Iraq. But French and German opposition to the war seriously undermined international credibility for the U.S. policy. It also complicated Bush administration efforts to bring international institutions and funding from other nations into the effort to stabilize and rebuild Iraq.

The Bush administration further undermined the image of the United States in Europe when, in September 2002, the White House released a policy statement on the "National Security Strategy of the United States." The paper focused on ". . . those terrorist organizations of global reach and any terrorist or state sponsor of terrorism which attempt to gain or use weapons of mass destruction (WMD) or their precursors." With regard to such threats, the document laid out an unambiguous strategy of preemption, saying "as a matter of common sense and self-defense, America will act against such emerging threats before they are fully formed."

Even though much of what the document said reflected realities of the contemporary security environment, it was interpreted widely in Europe as a unilateral assertion of rights beyond the accepted norms of international law that could be misused by the United States or copied by other countries, with destabilizing results.

European public opinion has been universally critical of what is seen as the unilateral use of U.S. power in Iraq. As a consequence, there is a significant democratic gap between all governments that have supported U.S. policies and their publics. Those governments that questioned or opposed U.S. policies have done so backed by strong popular support. Europe, whose fate was at the center of the Cold War, no longer is the central security concern for the United States. The challenge to European governments and to the United States is to make Europe a more effective part of the solution. In spite of profound differences over Iraq, there has been progress on both the organizational and the capabilities fronts. The United States and European nations have cooperated closely in dealing with terrorist threats. The members of the European Union have created the potential for the EU members to enhance their military cooperation in every area of defense endeavors, from strategic planning to weapons systems development to training and exercising to deployment of forces in combined and joint operations. The United States and its NATO allies have expanded NATO's mission and area of operation to give it important roles in the war on terrorism. The major European powers know what needs to be done to improve their military forces to be able to work and fight effectively alongside their U.S. ally. The question remains whether political leaders will provide sufficient resources for this to happen.

One of the most difficult tasks will be rebuilding the U.S. relationship with France, which was severely damaged by the Iraq debate. Not only did relations at the top levels of government suffer, but also public opinion in each of the two countries moved decisively against the other.

The U.S.-French relationship has never been, and may never be, the most comfortable that either country has in its ties with other nations. However, the fact is that U.S. and French interests in the world overlap more than they conflict. Moreover, the United States knows that France not only can make serious trouble for its foreign and defense policy goals from its position on the UN Security Council and as a leading member of the European Union but also can be a very helpful partner in dealing with future security challenges. In the latter regard, France's military capabilities and force projection mentality are second only to the United Kingdom among U.S. allies.

For its part, France knows it cannot achieve its foreign and defense policy goals in permanent opposition to the United States and that its interests are best served when the two countries cooperate, as they have recently tried to do concerning the crisis in Haiti. Both countries therefore have a strong mutual interest in moving beyond the Iraq crisis.

Implications in Asia

In Asia, public and elite opinion is similar to that in Europe. Popular opinion throughout Asia is deeply critical of U.S. policies. In a number of countries there is a generational divide, with younger Asians more angry at America than their parents. However, Asian governments have been much less vocal in opposition to recent U.S. unilateralism, judging that their domestic priorities and dependence on the United States for economic and security ties outweighs their concern about unilateral U.S. actions in areas of secondary concern like Iraq. Of much greater concern to many Asian governments is the crisis in North Korea, where—perhaps of necessity rather than preference—the Bush administration has followed a consultative approach involving other concerned powers that calms the crisis, though it does little to stop North Korea's development of nuclear weapons. Meanwhile, European governments and populations clearly feel a much larger stake than do Asian governments in the system of international law, organization, and cooperation that they see as threatened by unilateral U.S. behavior.

Reflecting secondary concern with Iraq and the Middle East, Asian relations with the United States have been less of a problem for the Bush administration than those with Europe. However, their secondary interest in Iraq and relative lack of experience in internal stabilization efforts means that Asian governments are also less likely to be a key part of the solution to the challenges facing the United States in Iraq and the broader Middle East and in the war on terrorism.

In the meantime, U.S. preoccupation with Southwest Asia clearly weakens U.S. leadership in other parts of Asia. U.S. policy has become very "reactive" in both Korea and Taiwan. So far no obvious harm has been done, but the United States is not well positioned to come up with coherent and effective strategies in Asia under these circumstances.

The next U.S. administration, whether led by George W. Bush or John Kerry, will face the challenge of developing a more coherent policy toward the Asian region that more effectively and actively protects and fosters U.S. interests in regional security, development, and democratization. Such an approach would require a clearer articulation of China's future role in the region, including the relationship between China and Taiwan, Japan's international role, the relevance of U.S. values of democracy and human rights in relations with Asian states, how to deal with the outstanding problems posed by the North Korean regime, and how to pursue U.S. economic interests in and strategy toward Asia. Such a comprehensive concept should also focus on how to engage Asian states in attempts to avoid future crises in their own region while contributing to efforts to deal with security challenges elsewhere, particularly in the Middle East.

The struggle against terror will require the active involvement and support of Asian governments. China plays an important role as a permanent member of the UN Security Council as well as a major emerging power in its own right. At present, China is engaged in a "charm offensive" in Asia, which led one observer recently to argue that Chinese foreign policy is more "interest based" at present in contrast to U.S. "threat based" policies. Japan and South Korea have the resources to contribute even more than they are already providing to international stability beyond their borders. U.S. policy will have to examine such questions in the light of broader U.S. interests in the region concerning the nature of the U.S. military presence and alliance relationships there. The United States will have to find the appropriate balance between Asia-specific interests and those driven by broader concerns about terrorism and international stability.

The Consequences of U.S. Unilateralism

The challenges of recouping the United States's eroding leadership position are captured in a statement made at a recent meeting in Washington by a prominent, retired Asian diplomat and friend of the United States. He said, "A post 9/11 environment and consequent unilateralist policies in Afghanistan and Iraq have created an image of the U.S. as a militaristic, egotistical, and brutal power which of course does not accord with the facts. Despite the U.S. enjoying unprecedented relations on the governmental level. Even in Northeast Asia, the people have a more negative view of the U.S. than at any other time in the past."4 The same could be said of the Middle East and of Europe.

With both Asian and European governments, the U.S. inclination toward preventive as well as preemptive military action in the wake of 9/11 has raised questions about the impact of these policies on international law, institutions, and multilateral relationships. The failures of U.S. intelligence and political judgment over Iraq have left many wondering how judicious the United States will be concerning the use of force in the future.

U.S. behavior, particularly the use of force without legitimacy provided by the UN Security Council, has so far not resulted in formal alliances against the United States and has not prevented U.S. administrations from taking steps they regarded as in the U.S. interest. In Asia, most governments have decided that it is not in their interest to be openly critical of the U.S.'s use of its power in the Middle East. European governments have been more willing to challenge U.S. policies and to seek to circumscribe U.S. power. Broadly, perceptions of the United States as a less-than-benign hegemonic power have

◆ limited the U.S. ability to build international coalitions in support of its foreign policy objectives, including the struggle against terror;

◆ turned public and elite opinion against the United States in key allied and partner states in Europe and Asia;

◆ weakened U.S. ability to use its "soft power" resources to help allied governments to make sacrifices in support of U.S. objectives;

◆ created electoral problems for some governments that chose to support U.S. initiatives, contributing to the electoral defeat of at least one friendly government (in Spain);

◆ undermined the cohesion of traditional bilateral and multilateral U.S. alliances, particularly NATO and the U.S.-South Korean alliance;

- jeopardized the long, post-World War II U.S. record of leadership in international organizations;

- further weakened the ability of the United Nations to deal with future threats to security;

- left the United States primarily responsible for what is proving to be a difficult and costly presence in Iraq;

- contributed to U.S. budget deficits that could threaten future U.S. economic well-being; and

- put heavy stress on U.S. regular, reserve, and National Guard forces and limited U.S. flexibility to deal with other possible security threats.

Generational Challenge

At the heart of the U.S. dilemma is a generational challenge. World War II and Cold War generations of European and Asian leaders are passing from the scene. They are being replaced by men and women whose feeling of gratitude to the United States is historical rather than personal. They lack commanding ideologies but bear allegiance to country and region and do not believe they should march to the tune of the U.S. drummer out of obligation. As a result, the challenge to persuade Asian and European publics of the necessity of U.S. policies is substantially greater than in the past. Moreover, looking forward, U.S. policymakers cannot rely on European and Asian governments to go against the wishes of their electorates, particularly when the credibility of America has been so tarnished by an Iraq war "case" built on faulty intelligence and suspect arguments.

This generational problem is, if anything, much greater in the Middle East and South Asia, where as much as 70 percent of the population is under the age of thirty. For many or most of these young people, America is the hyperpower that sustains failed secular leaders in their regions, underwrites Israel's brutal occupation, denigrates Islam, and utilizes its massive force as an instrument of humiliation.

On the Brink of Strategic Reversal

Now the United States finds itself, more than a year after the official end of the Iraq war, dangerously exposed in the Middle East—not just in Iraq but also in Afghanistan, in Pakistan, and with respect to Arab-Israeli peace. Its leverage with key allies in Europe and Asia have been weakened. The Bush administration has placed U.S. word and national prestige behind a "road map" for Arab-Israeli peace, democratic governance and stability in Afghanistan and Iraq, and an Iran without nuclear weapons. On all of these issues, U.S. policies are in deep trouble. The United States is now vulnerable to strategic reversal in the region. The gap between Washington's official rhetoric and on-the-ground performance is widening. The United States faces three potentially serious challenges arising out of its exposed Middle East/South Asia position:

◆ An expanding mismatch between U.S. commitments, on the one hand, and the U.S. human and financial resources necessary to sustain them on the other.

◆ The risk of a significant crisis elsewhere in the world—including a major attack at home—which could overwhelm the U.S.'s ability to respond. (The failure of the United States to be sufficiently attentive to looming challenges elsewhere was reinforced by news in May that North Korea may have transferred uranium to Libya, underscoring the proliferation challenges this regime poses for the world.)[5]

◆ The possibility that the American people will conclude that their country has become overcommitted in a volatile region and will demand withdrawal or a significant scaling back of commitments.

The United States, in short, is on the cusp of potential strategic failure in the Middle East/South Asia region, the ripple effects from which would be felt throughout Eurasia and beyond.

What would constitute such a "strategic failure"? Certainly being forced out of Iraq or seeing a collapse of order in Afghanistan would constitute abrupt failures, as might the assassination of President Musharraf of Pakistan or withdrawal of Iran from the Non-Proliferation Treaty. But, the United States is also vulnerable to the continuing violence between Palestinians and Israelis, which is sapping the U.S. position in the region.

It is remarkable and disturbing that in so many places terrorists and insurgencies are undermining stability and affecting outcomes—potentially delaying elections in Afghanistan and Iraq and successfully forestalling peace negotiations between Israelis and Palestinians. Indeed, it is possible to conclude that, since the U.S. invasion of Iraq, terrorists have mounted even more serious challenges to stability in the Middle East. Moderate regimes are at risk and their ties with the West in jeopardy throughout the region because association with America is dangerous.

America finds itself in the middle of religious and nationalist conflicts throughout the Middle East and South and Southeast Asia. It was not the U.S.'s desire to be part of these internal struggles. President Ronald Reagan extricated America from a similar conflict in Lebanon in the early 1980s; President Bush has been less successful thus far in limiting the U.S.'s involvement in the region and broadening the direct support of other governments for U.S. efforts.

Granted, President Bush confronts an unprecedented challenge—stateless fanatics with potential access to weapons of mass destruction. The 9/11 attacks did not lend themselves to prepackaged, preordained responses. Of necessity, U.S. policies needed to be constructed on the fly, mindful that more attacks on America could come at any time. Nonetheless, President Bush must be judged on his accomplishments. Has he secured America and furthered U.S. interests?

Implications for the Future

A highly optimistic scenario for U.S. policy in the Middle East would envision the emergence of a democratic and stable Iraq, a modernizing and more U.S.-friendly regime in Iran, decisive movement toward the peaceful establishment of a Palestinian state in the context of security guarantees for Israel, diminished popular support for radical Islamic terrorist groups and weakening of their ability to conduct significant operations, enhanced regional stability that reduces pressure for proliferation of weapons of mass destruction, and reinvigoration of U.S. alliances with European and Asian states and their involvement in UN-mandated operations designed to help preserve the peace in the Middle East and South Asia.

Such a hopeful scenario, however, appears unlikely to characterize the road immediately ahead. Instead, there are, it seems to us, two broad scenarios for the U.S.'s continuing involvement in the Middle East and in relations with its key European and Asian allies. Both begin with the possible future course of events in Iraq, the central challenge facing America today. But, each scenario identifies the consequences for U.S. power that accrue from our Iraqi engagement. Examination of these scenarios exposes what could happen and what needs to be done to forestall negative outcomes.

Scenario #1—"Muddle Through"

The United States might "succeed" in Iraq if success is defined only as stabilizing the situation and facilitating a full Iraqi assumption of sovereign control. It seems clear that achieving just this much will require significant effort. At an earlier stage, the United States had the option of introducing overwhelming force to achieve maximum control and coincidentally facilitate expanding Iraqi authority. At least the first half of that approach is probably no longer available. Indeed, the high point of U.S. power and authority in Iraq was passed some time ago. The United States in such a scenario would stop defining success as a "democratic" Iraq or an Iraq that permits a long-term U.S. troop presence. "Success" would be facilitating a transfer of authority to Iraqis without a breakup of the nation and without the new government's reverting to the brutal practices of the Saddam era. It is this option that the United States is pursuing with the official blessing of the United Nations. It remains to be seen whether the appointed Iraqi interim government can succeed.

The indigenous and external forces arrayed against this outcome are significant. The scramble for power among Iraqi factions will continue for the indefinite future. The hope is that responsible Iraqis, committed to a positive future for their country, will come out on top. What is clear is that to achieve even this minimal success the

United States will genuinely have to devolve power to Iraqis. The more prolonged the U.S. presence, the more Iraqis are likely to be driven to sympathize with resistance movements. The process of transferring genuine responsibilities to the Iraqis is now underway, but the challenges remain formidable. Some of Iraq's neighbors and radical opponents have direct stakes in promoting a failure of the U.S. experiment in "democracy promotion by force." Moreover, it remains unclear how much genuine assistance other outsiders—from the United Nations to Europeans—can provide in the face of most Iraqis' determination to chart their own course. Responsible Iraqis may in fact have to do so by denying their U.S., European, and UN sponsors in order to build credibility at home.

Beyond Iraq, the United States would have to attract additional help in dealing with the challenges of stabilizing Afghanistan, with a potentially nuclearizing Iran, and with the Palestinian/Israel conflict. It is difficult to project how this last problem could be turned to a more constructive direction. At present, the choices seem to be the following: an indefinitely continuing conflict, the Sharon withdrawal and fence construction approach, and the "Taba formula" leading to two viable and secure states. At a minimum, the Palestinians will have to be given confidence that negotiations rather than terrorism will give them a state of their own. It is hard to imagine that an Israeli-imposed solution will do so. The only alternative to continuing conflict remains a negotiated outcome. This conflict is not only a major source of U.S. problems in the Middle East but also a source of fundamental transatlantic differences.

The bottom line in this scenario is that U.S. power would be preserved but constrained by the need to work with others. Success would be defined as much by what is avoided as by what is achieved. Regrettably, reversals may be unavoidable at this late stage. This brings us to our second scenario.

Scenario # 2—"Strategic Failure"

The real debate today is whether the time has passed when the United States can succeed in the Middle East. It may well be that we must adjust to strategic failure as one or more of the U.S.'s initiatives crumble in the region, victim to naïve hopes and the internal forces of change exploding in countries across the region. If this proves the case, than damage control rather than enlargement of opportunities will be the challenge faced by the administration assuming office in January 2005.

According to a more pessimistic scenario, there may, in fact, be no winning strategy for the United States in Iraq. One definition of a viable nation is that the governing authority has a monopoly over the legitimate use of force within its borders. No such monopoly exists in a unified Iraq at present and may not in the foreseeable future. But the fundamental glue for a united Iraq may not be in place, as it was not in Yugoslavia or in the former Soviet Union. As the U.S. hand steadily lightens—particularly with continuing violence—the breakup of the nation may become inevitable. It may simply be that Iraq is not destined to be a unified state. In these circumstances, the U.S. presence would likely be untenable. The United States would leave Iraq in varying degrees of chaos and disrepair. The United States and its coalition allies would be left with the challenge of transferring their support from a united Iraq to one or more of its replacement states.

The ripple effects of U.S. failure could be significant. Terrorism would be perceived as successful. Moderate leaders identified with the United States from Pakistan to Morocco would be under pressure. America would be perceived as abandoning a commitment, however ill conceived and poorly pursued.

Less clear, but potentially significant, could be the reaction of allies and rivals in other regions. To the degree that the United States has been perceived as a stabilizing force in Europe and Asia, this role would be undercut. It is possible, in this pessimistic scenario, that North Korea or China might take advantage of our discomfiture to press their own agendas on nuclear weapons in the case of the DPRK and on Taiwan in the case of China.

Guidelines for the Future

The stakes are high in Iraq, but the best course of action is far from clear. To maintain sizable U.S. troop levels in Iraq reinforces those who label the United States an occupation regime. Precipitous withdrawal invites chaos in Iraq and the perception of vulnerability.

Clearly, the incoming administration must be prepared for uncertainty and a fluid Middle East scene in January 2005. Writing in June 2004, we cannot offer specific recommendations on next steps but rather guidelines within which particular policies should be framed. In 2004, as developments turned demonstrably against U.S. policy goals in Iraq, the Bush administration moved away from its strongly unilateralist posture and has been more open to international efforts in the region beyond the U.S.-led coalition in Iraq. (We are, we confess, reminded of Winston Churchill's pointed observation that "Americans can always be counted on to do the right thing . . . after they have exhausted all other possibilities.") The tendency to broaden responsibility in Iraq has to be reinforced, articulated clearly, and demonstrated by deeds as well as words. Our hope is that the "muddling through" scenario can succeed. Essential to success will be not only genuine U.S. withdrawal of authority, but also Iraqi forces of moderation stepping forward, a continuing positive and constructive posture on the part of our European friends, and the substantial engagement of UN agencies and personal.

The key element underlying any strategy must be sincere and credible efforts by the United States to involve other nations and international organizations in the process of stabilizing Iraq and the broader Middle East region. This includes increased reliance on the "Quad" diplomatic framework in which the United States, the European Union, Russia, and the United Nations collaborate to deal with the Israeli-Palestinian and related Middle East security issues. This said, the next administration must reach a fundamental decision with respect to the Israeli/Palestinian issue. The Sharon-driven, unilateral approach may dampen the violence, but it will not settle the conflict. Genuine revival of the process, which led to Taba during the Clinton administration, might expose the next president of the United States to domestic political risk but, if successful, could transform the U.S.'s image in the region.

Such cooperative approaches will require the United States and Europe to rebuild a constructive dialogue to replace the destructive interactions that have characterized handling of the Iraq issue. This would oblige the United States to follow President Theodore

Roosevelt's advice to "speak more softly," as everyone knows the United States already carries the "biggest stick." Future U.S. administrations will have to be more constructive and creative in the use of international institutions and multilateral cooperation. The United Nations, with all its shortcomings, remains a critical forum for legitimizing international security efforts. As has been demonstrated in Iraq, U.S. interests benefit when the United States can gain the international support and assistance that political legitimization that the United Nations brings.

For their part, Europeans will have to bring more resources and capabilities to the transatlantic security table. The U.S.-European relationship needs a better balance in terms of both authority and capability. It is not up to the United States, however, to "give" Europe more authority. European nations and the European Union will wield greater influence in Washington and internationally based on their will and ability to contribute to solutions of international security problems.

The next U.S. administration must make a clear and convincing commitment to use its power in ways that are compatible with international law, organizations, and cooperation with other democratic states. A new administration led by John Kerry would bring new leadership to key positions at the departments of State and Defense, and the National Security Council, and it also seems likely that a second Bush administration would see significant changes in leadership in these key positions. In either case, the United States cannot afford serious discontinuities in efforts to set U.S. policy on a more successful course than the one followed in recent years. We know now that "style" matters. A leadership that denigrates international organizations and friends in the good times cannot count on their support in periods of difficulty.

Top priorities for U.S. foreign policy must be building and sustaining broadly based international coalitions in support of the struggle against terror, in favor of limiting the proliferation of weapons of mass destruction, and on behalf of a just peace between Israel and the Palestinians. But, we also believe that America faces a more profound challenge. U.S. policies must address not only the dangers posed by enemies of order and progress but must also speak to the aspirations of new generations emerging around the world for whom America may no longer be viewed as a source of hope and compassion. The United States must earn that trust and confidence again.

The Congress of the United States, which avoided taking responsibility for going to war against Iraq, should reestablish itself as a true partner for the executive branch in the formulation of U.S. foreign and defense policy, offering critical advice and judgments when necessary and support and resources when warranted.

In the end, America cannot withdraw from the world. The United States cannot, in its own self-interest, extricate itself from geopolitical responsibility. U.S. leaders have to be smarter about how America conducts itself around the world. U.S. administrations clearly need to understand the differences between conflict and post-conflict and how we meet the challenges of the latter without scrimping on the responsibilities of the former. Leaders need to be rigorous in matching resources—financial and human—to the tasks the United States takes on. Finally, the United States needs to maintain a realistic appreciation of what is possible and not lay out goals that expose gaps between U.S. promises and performance.

Even if the next administration follows such guidance, the task will not be easy. Moving back from the brink of strategic reversal in the Middle East could take years of patient policymaking and a long-term commitment to the costs of peacekeeping and reconstruction efforts. The image of the United States as a marauding hegemon, which undermines the U.S.'s ability to achieve its many objectives in the world, will take years of cooperative, constructive behavior to change.

The United States will not always be able to respond to international security challenges with multilateral approaches. There will be times when unilateral responses or even preemptive actions are required. However, such cases should be the exception, not the rule. The United States will remain the only true global power for the foreseeable future. The challenge will be to manage that power in ways that advance U.S. interest by building coalitions among like-minded peoples and governments around the globe.

Notes

1. G. John Ikenberry, "Strategic Reactions to American Preeminence: Great Power Politics in the Age of Unipolarity" (Washington, D.C.: National Intelligence Council, July 28, 2003), 2.

2. Corey Robin, "Grand Designs—How 9/11 Unified Conservatives in Pursuit of Empire," *Washington Post*, May 2, 2004, B1.

3. Thomas E. Ricks, "80% of Iraq Distrust Occupation Authority," *Washington Post*, May 13, 2004, A10.

4. Delivered at a not-for-attribution meeting convened by The Asia Foundation in Washington, D.C., on May 14, 2004.

5. See David E. Sanger, "The North Korea Uranium Challenge," *New York Times*, May 24, 2004.

2

U.S. Power and Influence in the Middle East and South Asia

CASIMIR A. YOST

President George H.W. Bush (the forty-first president) was a transitional figure. He entered his presidency confronting the Soviet Union and exited it dispatching U.S. troops to Somalia. On his watch, America went from superpower confrontation to peacekeeping.

President Bush drew on a lifetime of experience to assemble an international coalition, acting under UN authority, to respond to Iraq's invasion of Kuwait in the summer of 1990. He selected a limited objective in ousting Saddam Hussein from Kuwait but choosing not to occupy Baghdad. The former president argued, in a book he cowrote with his former national security adviser, Brent Scowcroft, that "[H]ad we gone the invasion route, the United States could conceivably still be an occupying power in a bitterly hostile land. It would have been a dramatically different—and perhaps barren—outcome."[1]

Twelve years later, his son reversed this decision, not only ordering the occupation of Iraq but also the significant expansion of the U.S. military presence throughout the Middle East and South Asia region. Bush (the forty-third president) committed America to rebuilding Iraq and Afghanistan and to the political transformation of the Middle East.

The proximate reason for this dramatic expansion of the U.S.'s role in the region was the challenge posed by Islamic terrorism and the September 11, 2001, attacks in New York and Washington, DC. But conviction that dramatic political change in the region was both

---

*This chapter was prepared with the participation of Stanley R. Sloan and Robert G. Sutter.

essential and possible played a role in the decisionmaking of George W. Bush and his senior advisers. The direct and indirect consequences of the accelerated intrusion of U.S. power into this region are unfolding as this is written. This chapter will—after some preliminary context-setting comments—focus on the evolving U.S. position in the original heartland of Islam.

The following two chapters deal with contemporary U.S. roles in Europe and Asia. Taken together, these three chapters examine the U.S. position in the Eurasian land mass in the first decade of the twenty-first century. In the words of Professor Robert J. Art, "Eurasia is home to most of the world's people, most of its major military powers, as well as a large share of its economic growth."[2] America's success or failure in this geographic expanse will help determine whether the American people will be secure in the decades ahead.

The following propositions underline the analysis in this paper:

- ◆ At the dawn of the twenty-first century, forces are converging in some regions of the world that have further weakened the nation-state as a locus of authority and stability.

- ◆ Nowhere is this more true than in the broad band of countries from Morocco to the Philippines—a region where globalization has provided uneven benefits, a huge youthful underclass has emerged, secular leadership has been broadly discredited, and radicalism is struggling with forces of moderation in Islam.

- ◆ It is a region where fundamental U.S. interests are engaged—because of oil and terrorism—but it is also a region where America risks becoming party to a civilizational struggle.

- ◆ The United States has successfully used the military means in the region to achieve defined military objectives but not political goals. U.S.-mobilized "coalitions of the willing" are proving inadequate in addressing postconflict challenges. Political goals in Israel/Palestine, in Iraq, in Iran, in Afghanistan (and one could add Pakistan) remain sadly elusive.

- ◆ America's contemporary intrusion into the Middle East/South Asia leaves it dangerously exposed to reversal and without substantial regional and international support. The United States is, at this moment, especially unprepared to manage a major crisis elsewhere in the world.

◆ The United States finds itself in the fourth year of the twenty-first century facing deeply critical, even antagonistic, publics not only in the Middle East/South Asia but in Europe and Asia as well. The legitimacy of U.S. policies is broadly questioned.

◆ The consequences of U.S. failure in the Middle East are unknowable at present but potentially serious. The road to success is similarly far from clear.

Background

America's active role in the Middle East did not begin with September 11, 2001, or with the 1991 Gulf War, for that matter. It began with missionary educators in the nineteenth century. These were followed by oil men and diplomats in the decades after World War II. The U.S. regional military presence remained modest and largely "over the horizon" until 1990. Bases in North Africa were closed decades ago. U.S. influence was built on relationships with congenial Middle Eastern and South Asian autocrats. Once the United States found them to be willing partners, it was uncritical of their domestic practices—however repressive. Washington was interested in regional counterweights to Soviet power and in the assured flow of oil from the region to world markets.

What changed? The following seem important: the collapse of the Soviet Union, the crystallized primacy of U.S. power, the rise of militant Islam, and the youth "bulge" in the region. None, with the exception of the first, represented a sharp discontinuity with the past. The U.S. military buildup, of course, began in the early 1980s. Militant Islam saw clear expression in the 1979 overthrow of the shah of Iran and the rise of Hezbollah in Lebanon in the 1980s. Demographic pressures obviously have been building for a long time. But all of these factors converged in the 1990s. Taken together, they contributed to a weakening of state authority in the Middle East/South Asia without fostering alternative sources of order and stability. Let us briefly touch on each:

Collapse of the Soviet Union. The geopolitical ripple effects from the precipitous collapse of the U.S.S.R. continue to be felt. America and the West lost a unifying enemy. Alliance bickering is no longer muted by fear of Soviet power. As important, perhaps, are the weak and weakened states left after the demise of the U.S.S.R. In Central Europe, relatively stable nations have arisen but not so in the Central Asian republics. A band of very weak states now exists from Georgia to Kyrgyzstan. Moreover, countries from Mongolia to North Korea to Cuba, which long relied on Soviet patronage and subsidized energy, no longer can do so. Some have embarked on substantial political and/or economic reform, but many have descended into despotism or economic decline. In the Middle East/South Asia, the absence of the Soviet threat removed a central measure by which the United States distinguished friends from enemies in the region.

United States primacy. John Ikenberry is right in saying that "American global power—military, economic, technological, cultural and political—is one of the great realities of our age."[3] But he is also right in saying the "the loss of the Cold War threat has removed bipolar restraints on American power."[4] During the Cold War, the United States was a defender of the status quo, linking itself to authoritarian regimes as well as to established democracies.

Containment of Soviet and, to a lesser degree, Chinese power was the central organizing focus of U.S. foreign policy. With the end of the Cold War and the removal of the Soviet military threat and a diminished Japanese economic challenge, the United States became a dominant if sometimes unsettling presence on the world scene, while also coincidentally being a stabilizing force through its markets, investments, aid, and global security presence. Americans proclaimed that their values—democracy and free markets—were or should be universal. The U.S. military intrusion into the Middle East became direct and forceful in 1990 in response to Iraq's invasion of Kuwait.

Militant Islam. There is a war in process within Islam, with radical elements, argues Daniel Philpott, "questioning the very legitimacy of the international order, the Westphalian synthesis, in all of its stands."[5] (Islam is not unique—fundamentalist Hindus and Jews also press exclusionary agendas driven by religious fervor immune from concern for consequences.) At the most extreme is Al-Qaeda, which challenges the nation-state system and seeks a pan-Islamic caliphate achieved through violence. Al-Qaeda has a central purpose: to undermine state authority everywhere with the rare exception of those states that temporarily offer its people sanctuary, as did Afghanistan under the Taliban.

Demographics. Half the world's population is under twenty-five years of age. "Youth bulges" exist in many poor regions of the world. It is estimated, according to Anthony Cordesman, that in North Africa and the Middle East, "[S]ome 70% of the population already is under 30 years of age and some 50% is under 20."[6] These are frequently unemployed and under-educated citizens, in their teens and twenties, with little hope of personal betterment. A National Intelligence Council (NIC) study estimates that between 2000 and 2015, Pakistan's population will grow from 140 million to 195 million, placing huge pressures on any Pakistani government—democratic or authoritarian.

How then do these factors come together? Clearly, the fear of Russian power is no longer of central importance in the Middle East/ South Asia, though it is in Central Asia and the Caucauses. U.S. power, both hard and soft, is a factor. Osama bin Laden's initial charge against the Saudi monarchy was that the royal family let the infidel enter the kingdom at the time of the Gulf War. Across the region from Morocco to Pakistan (and on to Southeast Asia) secular authority has struggled with Islamic impulses. In some cases, including in Algeria, this struggle has been very violent. The common reality in much of the region has been the failure of secular leadership to provide for either the material or political aspirations of the citizens of their countries. Fast-expanding populations, or "youth bulges," have exacerbated this problem. The identification of regional leaders with the increasingly unpopular superpower has further undermined central governments in the region.

Pakistan and Saudi Arabia showcase the impact of these pressures, which were worsened by decades of bad leadership in both countries. In both Pakistan and Saudi Arabia, Islamic influences on government decisionmaking are greater than thirty years ago, personal liberty and individual choice are lower, corruption has increased, and domestic security has declined significantly. By virtually any measure, most Pakistani and Saudi citizens are not better off today than they were three decades ago. Moreover, thanks to the information revolution, they know it. This matters because, in the words of Robert Rothberg, "Weak states typically harbor ethnic, religious, linguistic, or other tensions that may at some near point be transformed into all out conflict between contending antagonisms."7

Prelude to Bush "43"

In the aftermath of the 1991 Gulf War, President George H.W. Bush committed the United States to an expanded security presence in the Persian Gulf, including the stationing of U.S. forces in Kuwait and Saudi Arabia, and initiated what came to be known as the "dual containment" policy intended to restrict and deter Iraq and Iran. He also worked for a settlement of the Arab-Israeli conflict. His foreign policy legacy, to his less-experienced successor, was to include not only a diminished Russia and a united Germany, but also unfinished business in Somalia, the Balkans, and the Middle East.

President Bill Clinton's initial focus and expertise were on domestic issues. His foreign policy interests were heavily weighted toward international economic issues. His early accomplishments included conclusion of the North American Free Trade Agreement (NAFTA) and World Trade Organization (WTO) agreements. He stumbled badly in Somalia, largely ignored genocide in Rwanda, and initially moved hesitantly in the Balkans.

Clinton's first national security adviser, Anthony Lake, defined the central thrust of U.S. foreign policy in the post-Cold War era as expanding the community of "free market democracies." In practice, over two terms, President Clinton focused considerable attention on conflicts in the Balkans, on expansion of NATO to the east, and on improving ties with China. In all three areas, following shaky early moves, he registered successes.

On President Clinton's watch, however, the United States gained power and lost influence. The collapse of the Soviet Union, the long-term Japanese economic slump, and remarkable U.S. economic growth, which Clinton's policies helped foster, put the United States in a position of unprecedented strength. Power, however, did not equate with influence. Other nations were respectful of the U.S.'s size but not of its authority. The U.S.'s failings were captured in the unfinished business President Clinton passed on to his successor:

◆ Dual containment of Iraq and Iran was largely defunct as an effective policy when President Clinton left office. As became clear in 2003, Iran had a robust, covert nuclear program underway. Furthermore, as the *New York Times* editorialized, "By 2001, Baghdad was collecting as much as $1 billion a year in illicit oil revenues."[8] Weapons inspectors had not visited Iraq since 1998, and many nations were pressing for a lifting of sanctions on one or both countries.

◆ The Middle East peace process had effectively collapsed by 2001, with the election of Ariel Sharon as Israel's prime minister and the commencement of the Palestinian terror campaign. The Middle East peacemaking challenge President Clinton bequeathed to his successor was unprecedented in its complexity precisely because core differences between Israelis and Palestinians were exposed as never before, and leaders were in place on both sides who were unprepared to overcome these differences to achieve a comprehensive and final agreement. (To say this should in no way diminish the very considerable personal attention and effort President Clinton gave to Middle East peacemaking.)

◆ The Clinton administration's failures on the nuclear proliferation front were huge—India and Pakistan became declared nuclear states on Clinton's watch and, we know now, North Korea was cheating on the 1994 Agreed Framework the administration had negotiated. The proliferation challenges the United States faced in 2001 were vastly more complex than a decade earlier, because two South Asian nations had "gone nuclear" and had, in many respects, been rewarded for doing so with—particularly in the case of India—improved relations with the United States.

◆ Finally, and most disturbing, the Clinton administration's failure to respond effectively to repeated Al-Qaeda attacks in the

1990s presumably emboldened Osama bin Laden and provided the setup for 9/11.⁹

Bush "43"

Woodrow Wilson said shortly after he was elected president in 1912 on a domestic platform, "What an irony of fate it would be if my administration was forced to devote its attention mainly to foreign policy." Wilson, of course, took the United States into World War I and failed to take it into the League of Nations.

The 2000 presidential campaign was contested primarily on domestic issues. Nonetheless, during the campaign, and certainly during the early months of George W. Bush's administration, Bush and his advisers made fundamental foreign policy distinctions with the Clinton administration. Generally, Bush defined U.S. national interests more narrowly, with greater attention given to preserving national sovereignty and expanding national power (in contrast to trends in Europe and, to a lesser degree in Asia, where acceptance of diminished sovereignty in an interdependent world is more widespread).

John Bolton, who subsequently became Undersecretary of State in the Bush administration, leveled a broadside attack at multilateralism in a 2000 article in the *Chicago Journal of International Law* entitled "Should We Take Global Governance Seriously?" Bolton argued, "It is well past the point when the unrestrained and uncritical acceptance of globalist slogans ('global solutions for global problems') can be allowed to proceed. The costs to the United States—reduced constitutional autonomy, impaired popular sovereignty, reduction of our international power, and limitations on our domestic and foreign policy options and solutions—are far too great, and the current understanding of these costs far too limited to be acceptable."¹⁰

These sentiments became operational when President Bush took office and in his first year in office rejected several cooperative agreements that had had the explicit or tacit support of his predecessor and widespread international support. These agreements included the International Criminal Court, the Kyoto Global Warming Protocol, and the Comprehensive Test Ban Treaty.

Bush advisers also derided what they saw as the Clinton administration's enthusiasm for "nation building" and particularly the use of U.S. armed forces to achieve this end. Bush campaign adviser and later national security adviser, Condoleezza Rice wrote in a 2000 *Foreign Affairs* article, "The president must remember that the military is a special instrument. It is lethal, and it is meant to be. It is not a civilian police force. It is not a political referee. And it is most certainly not designed to build a civilian society."[11] Of course, every new administration seeks to distinguish itself from its predecessor. Experience in office invariably tempers campaign rhetoric.

As always, organizing to manage foreign policy was a challenge. Administrations now take a year or more to get their people in place, given expanding confirmation process hurtles. Authority over foreign policy is spread across many departments of government. In the 1990s, the balance of power on foreign affairs had shifted from the executive toward the legislative branch. The Department of State was weakened by budget cuts, uneven leadership, and President Clinton's heavy reliance on his national security adviser in his second term.

President Bush placed strong individuals in cabinet positions in Defense and State and appointed a trusted, but a relatively less experienced, individual as his national security adviser. Importantly, he vested more foreign policy authority in his vice president than had any president in history. But, as the summer of 2001 unfolded, it was unclear how this "team" would mesh and what concrete priorities would emerge from the somewhat chaotic early months of the administration.

September 11, 2001

The attacks on the World Trade Center and the Pentagon initiated an unprecedented discontinuity in the U.S. foreign policy continuum. The consequences flowing from these attacks will affect America and her interests for years to come.

An American president has no greater responsibility than to protect the United States from assault at home. In September 2001, the American people were successfully attacked at home by a foreign enemy and, critically, it was suggested that more and even more destructive attacks could come at any time. The Bush administration in its early months had been no more successful in dealing with the Al-Qaeda threat than had the Clinton administration. In fact, confronting that threat appeared to be a low priority on the administration's early agenda.

The actions of nineteen individuals and those who dispatched them transformed an American president, dramatically reordered a superpower's priorities and regional focus, significantly shifted U.S. budgetary priorities, and resulted in a major expansion of the U.S. global military presence, thrusting America into first defeating and then rebuilding Afghanistan and Iraq. Implicit in all that has happened since 9/11 is that the United States finds itself at war with a radical element in the Islamic world.

The intellectual underpinnings of the Bush administration's redefinition of U.S. foreign policy after September 11 are captured in the White House-produced document entitled *National Security Strategy of the United States,* issued in September 2002. This document argues that "America is now threatened less by conquering states than we are by failing ones." It warns that "[T]he gravest danger our Nation faces lies at the crossroads of radicalism and technology." Most controversially, it states that "as a matter of common sense and self-defense, America will act against such emerging threats before they are fully formed." The report goes on to say: "Our immediate focus will be those terrorist organizations of global reach and any terrorist or state sponsor of terrorism which attempts to gain or use weapons of mass destruction (WMD) or their precursors." Then, in another phrase, which has captured much attention, the document states: "While the United States will constantly strive to enlist the support of the international community we will not hesitate to act alone, if necessary, to exercise our right of self-defense by acting preemptively against such terrorists. . . ."[12]

The Bush administration put aside old norms in the face of a new enemy, without a precise street address, operating with new weapons. "Containment" and "deterrence," which characterized U.S. security policies in the Cold War, were replaced by "forward defense" and the possibility of "preemption." National attention was turned from concern with big powers to a focus on poor, weak states. Russia and China were winners, and Mexico, Europe, and East Asia losers as U.S. foreign policy refocused on the broad swath of countries stretching from Morocco to the Philippines—home to Islam, modern terrorism, and WMD in unsteady hands.

The rewards and perils of the U.S.'s reorientation are all too evident in South Asia and the Middle East.

Afghanistan/Pakistan

The Bush administration's approach to the post-9/11 world was revealed in its actions with respect to Afghanistan and Pakistan.

President Bush directed the use of U.S. military power and intelligence assets to defeat an enemy. His administration was prepared to take risks to achieve its objectives. In the case of Afghanistan, these risks included putting small numbers of U.S. special forces on the ground and relying on air power, precision munitions and often unsavory Northern Alliance allies to win. The administration also showed an early preference for "coalitions of the willing" versus reliance on established, treaty-based alliances. Secretary of Defense Donald Rumsfeld said, "Wars can benefit from coalitions of the willing, to be sure, but they should not be fought by committee. The mission must determine the coalition, the coalition must not determine the mission."

But, the administration's commitment to bringing the war to a rapid and successful conclusion was not matched by its commitment to rebuilding Afghanistan into a viable and strengthening state. Put bluntly, the administration's verbal pledge to rebuild Afghanistan exceeded its on-the-ground commitment of resources and personnel. The administration was unprepared to take on the security responsibilities essential to rebuilding a stable Afghanistan, and so more than two years after the successful defeat of the Taliban, security and reconstruction remain faltering in Afghanistan. The economy survives on the drug trade, which in turn props up the warlords and, presumably, the remnants of Al-Qaeda and the Taliban. Journalist Ahmed Rashid points out: "In 2003, Afghanistan produced 3,600 tons of opium or 76 percent of total world production."[13] The central government in Kabul is starved for resources, and the United Nations warns that "there is a palpable risk that Afghanistan will again turn into a failed state, this time in the hands of drug cartels and narco-terrorists."[14]

The Bush administration also rapidly transformed U.S.-Pakistan relations from quasi-hostile pre-9/11 to a quasi partnership since then. This "partnership" has proved unsatisfactory for both sides. Pakistani leaders have been of significant assistance in the war on terrorism, but their limitations have been all too evident in the relative safe haven provided Taliban (and Al-Qaeda) fighters in the areas of Pakistan bordering Afghanistan. Much depends on the continued survival of President Pervez Musharraf, who has walked a fine line between meeting U.S. demands on terrorism and proliferation issues while bowing to popular sentiment in Pakistan that is deeply skeptical of the United States. The delicacy of Musharraf's position became all too evident when two major assassination efforts against him failed and when revelations emerged that a prominent Pakistani scientist, Dr. A.Q. Khan, ran a WMD trading network that sent bomb-making designs and equipment to Iran, North Korea, and Libya and quite possibly other countries. The irony, of course, is that the United States invaded Iraq to prevent it from becoming a WMD proliferator, only to discover that Pakistan, an ally in the war on terrorism, had become a WMD trading hub.

The challenge facing the Bush administration is that post-9/11 U.S. interests are closely tied to two very fragile South Asian states. The stability of both Afghanistan and Pakistan depend heavily on the continuation in power of leaders who have narrowly escaped assassination attempts. There are, therefore, limitations with respect to what the United States can expect of or demand from both President Musharraf of Pakistan and President Hamid Karzai of Afghanistan. Yet, decisive failure in either country would pose great risks for both the U.S. war on terrorism and U.S. efforts to control the proliferation of weapons of mass destruction.

Important successes, of course, have been registered against the Al-Qaeda leadership. Indeed, the Bush administration can take credit for significantly expanding cooperation with intelligence agencies around the world. This said, the *New York Times* noted in February, "The landscape of the terrorist threat has shifted, many intelligence officials around the world say, with more than a dozen regional militant Islamic groups showing signs of growing strength and broader ambitions, even as the operational power of Al-Qaeda appears diminished."[15] Terrorist bombings from Bali, to Istanbul, to Casablanca, to Madrid send a chilling message about the spreading activity of bin Laden's offspring. The escalating terrorist attacks in Saudi Arabia are particularly worrisome given the kingdom's aging and divided leadership and the potential for a severe disruption of the world's energy markets that could result from a spectacular attack in that country. U.S. invasions first of Afghanistan and then of Iraq are helping to rally the faithful against the infidel in Saudi Arabia and elsewhere.

Iraq

Almost ninety years ago, British General Stanley Maude captured Baghdad from the Ottomans and proclaimed, "Our armies do not come into your cities and lands as conquerors or enemies, but as liberators." It took decades for Iraqis to completely rid their country of British power. Americans may have forgotten this history—Iraqis have not.

President George W. Bush implicitly rejected the cautionary comments of his father about the risks of the United States becoming "an occupying power in a bitterly hostile land" and chose to remove Saddam Hussein and his Baathist government from power. The application of U.S. combat power to defeat an enemy was brilliantly executed. The war began March 19, 2003, and by mid-April was essentially over. The capture of Saddam Hussein in December 2003 signaled that a vicious tyrant would never again trouble his people and the region. There should be no question that Iraq is better off for Saddam's defeat. The unanswered question is whether larger U.S. interests were served by this war, fought at this time, in this way.

The ongoing debate with respect to Iraq cannot be fully addressed here, but some general observations are appropriate. Richard Haass, who was director of policy planning for the State Department for the first two and a half years of the Bush administration, wrote about the Iraq war that "at its core it was a war of choice. We did not have to go to war against Iraq, certainly not when we did."[16]

The distinction between preemption and prevention is relevant. Scholars Charles Kegley Jr. and Gregory A. Raymond argue that "[A] *preemptive* military attack entails the use of force to quell or mitigate an impending strike by an adversary. A *preventive* military attack entails the use of force to eliminate any possible future strike, even when there is not reason to believe that aggression is planned or the capability to launch such an attack is operational."[17] By this definition, Operation Iraqi Freedom was—it is now clear—a preventive war, even though it was sold as an urgent preemptive action at the time it was launched.

The administration sought international legitimacy through the United Nations but did so in a halfhearted way. The *Financial Times* (London) had it right: "The measure of this diplomatic fiasco is that a perfectly arguable case about one of the most despicable dictators of modern times was so mishandled that public opinion internationally came to worry more about the misuse of U.S. power than about Saddam Hussein." The irony is that by some measures, President Bush was hugely successful. He succeeded in refocusing the world's attention on the threat posed by Saddam Hussein and succeeded in getting UN inspectors reintroduced into Iraq.

We can only speculate whether a more robust diplomatic effort and greater flexibility on the part of the Bush administration might have achieved broader international backing as well as UN support in the form of a second resolution and more coalition partners in the fight to come. It is worth recalling that following Iraq's invasion of Kuwait in 1990, then Secretary of State James Baker made thirty-nine stops on five trips between September 1990 and January 1991 building a coalition to evict Iraq from Kuwait. No comparable effort was made in 2002–03.

We know now that the intelligence used to buttress the case for war was badly flawed. Kenneth Pollack, a former National Security Council staffer who supported the effort to oust Saddam Hussein, wrote: "The intelligence community did overestimate the scope and progress of Iraq's WMD programs although not to the extent that many people believe. The Administration stretched those estimates to make a case not only for going to war but for doing so at once, rather than taking the time to build regional and international support for military action."[18]

Administration leaders hyped what they knew. On September 19, 2002, Secretary of Defense Donald Rumsfeld stated flatly, "No terrorist state poses a greater or more immediate threat to the security of our people than the regime of Saddam Hussein and Iraq."[19] But, in fairness, this was hardly the first instance of an administration exaggerating a case to build support for a preferred policy. Dean Acheson, Secretary of State under President Truman, in discussing the task of a public officer seeking to explain and gain support for a major policy, wrote: "Qualification must give way to simplicity of statement, nicety and nuance to bluntness, almost brutality in carrying home a point . . . points to be understandable had to be clear. If we made our points clearer than truth, we did not differ from most other educators and could hardly do otherwise."[20] This said, the Bush administration's "case" for war was built on weapons of mass destruction that did not exist and on unproven Iraqi ties to Al-Qaeda. As a result, U.S. credibility has been dangerously undermined.

What, in retrospect, was totally unacceptable was the failure to plan for what would come after the war in Iraq. Vice President Richard Cheney's much-quoted comment on *Meet the Press* three days before hostilities commenced—"I really do believe that we will be greeted as liberators"—captured a dangerous administration mindset. Many in and out of government warned that governing postconflict Iraq would not be easy, but they were largely ignored. The civilians in the Pentagon remained focused on the lean force necessary to win the battle, not the robust force essential to securing the peace. They literally froze out of the decision process people in other agencies who argued that postconflict reconstruction in Iraq would not be a cakewalk. In retrospect, the U.S. failure to secure Turkish approval for the army's Fourth Infantry Division to open a northern front in Iraq was significant. This failure meant that the United States lacked a robust force capable of rapidly stabilizing Iraq and imposing order once major combat operations were over.

U.S. forces in Iraq were forced to take on tasks for which they were neither properly trained nor properly equipped. Today the army, national guard, and reserves are being badly stretched by the heavy demands placed on them by requirements in Iraq.

Further, the determination to proceed to fight with a narrow "coalition of the willing" meant that the United States was left with the overwhelming responsibility for postconflict reconstruction and its costs, human and financial. The visible disdain for the United Nations and a number of traditional allies, evidenced by certain administration officials, also undermined efforts to broaden participation in the postwar phase.

Members of the Bush administration have never been candid in public about the possible "costs" of the decision to oust Saddam Hussein. There can be no doubt that the invasion of Iraq diverted resources—human and financial—from other critical priorities. Jeffrey Record, in a report published by the Army War College, argues that "[T]he result has been an unnecessary preventative war of choice against a deterred Iraq that has created a new front in the Middle East for Islamic terrorism and diverted attention and resources away from securing the American homeland against further assault by an undeterrable Al-Qaeda. The war against Iraq was not integral to the (Global War on Terror), but rather a detour from it."[21] Bush administration policymakers profoundly disagree. They argue that a powerful and essential statement has been made to terrorists and to state leaders tempted to aid them or otherwise "challenge" the United States.

Deputy Secretary of Defense Paul Wolfowitz put the dilemma faced by policymakers as follows: "In the end, it has to come down to a careful weighing of things we can't know with precision, the costs of action versus the costs of inaction, the costs of action now versus the costs of action later."[22] One could argue as well that if, on balance it was prudent to go to war, then too it would have been prudent to prepare more effectively for what followed the war.

The United States was unprepared to handle the chaos that followed the occupation of Iraq. The looting and destruction caught U.S. leaders by surprise. Serious errors of judgment ensued, including the decision to fully disband the Iraqi army, which was, according to retired Lieutenant General Jay Garner and the chief of the initial reconstruction team in Iraq, "a huge, huge mistake."[23] Pauline Baker, at the Fund for Peace, argues, "In a brilliant demonstration of the law of unintended consequences, the U.S.-led invasion of Iraq went far beyond its original goal of regime change. It precipitated the final collapse of a state that had been deteriorating for years. Shattered states proliferate, not eliminate, threats, however, and that is exactly what happened in Iraq."[24]

As this is written, the United States has initiated three transitions simultaneously—a transition of sovereignty to Iraqi government control of the state to occur June 30, 2004, a security transition to new Iraqi forces to occur over the coming months, and coalition troop rotations. Each is filled with uncertainty and challenge. None is assured.

U.S. influence in the region peaked when U.S. forces entered Baghdad in April 2003. That was the time the United States needed overwhelming force to secure the peace, set the U.S.'s mark on Iraq's future, and give hope to the prospect of a positive future for a unified Iraq. The United States lost that opportunity and has witnessed the erosion of its influence in Iraq ever since. The United States, we know now, had a limited opportunity to improve the lives of ordinary Iraqis and to set the country on a positive course. The initiative is now in the hands of others—terrorists and clerics. Iraqi insurgents are defining themselves in the eyes of increasing numbers of Iraqis not as enemies of freedom, as President Bush suggests, but as enemies of occupation. Larry Diamond, who served as an adviser to the Coalition Provisional Authority, summed up the situation in May 2004 as follows, "More and more Iraqis have been coming around to the view that if we cannot give them security, jobs, and electricity, why should they continue to suffer the general humiliation and countless specific indignities of American forces occupying their land."25

The setting of June 30 as the date for transfer of political authority—without clarity as to who would take on that authority—persuaded many Iraqis that the United States was winding down its occupation and that political forces in Iraq should move smartly to position themselves for what might happen.

On June 8, 2004, the UN Security Council voted unanimously in favor of a resolution ending the formal occupation of Iraq on June 30 and passing full sovereignty to an interim, appointed Iraqi government. The resolution lays out a process leading to a permanent, elected Iraqi government to take office on January 31, 2006.

The intervening months cannot help but be troubled. The interim government may not be viewed as more legitimate than the Iraqi governing council it is replacing. The debate about what constitutes "full sovereignty" will continue. The volatile mix of coalition forces, emerging Iraqi security forces, proliferating militias, and outside extremists cannot make anyone sanguine that sufficient stability will exist to get on with the reconstruction of the country and holding national elections by January 2005. Moreover, we know that the gap between Kurdish hopes for autonomy and Shiite aspirations for authority befitting their majority status will not be easily bridged.

Regrettably, the likely scenarios for Iraq's immediate future are not pretty—a breakup of the nation with Iraq's neighbors supporting favorites, or a weak center and distinct semi-autonomous regions subject to outside interference, or a renewed authoritarian central authority. The UN resolution posits a functioning democracy in a stable state—a wonderful but unlikely outcome. What seems clear is that increasingly Iraqis will demand to take charge of their own future and shape that future in their own way.

The dilemma, of course, for the United States is that its armed forces are to be present—albeit with diminished authority—as Iraqis sort out the future shape of their country and the manner in which it is governed. This will, if anything, be a larger challenge for the U.S. than any to date in this troubled land.

Israel-Palestine

Columnist Tom Friedman wrote in January 2004, "Let's not mince words. American policy today toward the Israeli-Palestinian conflict is insane."[26]

In December 2003, the *New York Times* reported that "[T]he Israeli Interior Ministry released figures on Tuesday showing that the number of Jewish settlers in the West Bank and the Gaza Strip had increased by 16 percent in the last three years, to 236,381—about double the number that existed when Israel signed the Oslo Accords in 1993."[27] Palestinian terrorism meanwhile continues to kill and maim innocent Israelis with the approval and support of Yasir Arafat. Prime Minister Sharon's response has been brutal in return—while he has begun work on a fence that will further divide and isolate Palestinians on the West Bank. More recently, he moved in the direction of a unilateral Israeli withdrawal from Gaza but has encountered resistance to his plans in his own party.

The likely result of this unfolding process will be to leave millions of Palestinians in Gaza and the West Bank without moderate leadership and without hope. "The complete collapse of the Palestinian Authority, which may be imminent," argues Henry Siegman, "would very probably rule out the two-state option, for there would be no central authority capable of delivering a Palestinian commitment to—much less the implementation of—the terms of any Israeli-Palestinian peace accord."[28] In practice, this means that Israel will control a Palestinian Arab population that shortly will exceed the Jewish population of Israel.

The Bush administration has shown sporadic, inconsistent, and largely ineffectual interest in the issue. Yet, through the footage and commentary of Al-Jeezera, the U.S. image and interests have been undermined throughout the Islamic world as Muslims have assumed that Sharon's actions could only occur with U.S. acquiescence. The Bush administration's assumptions seem to be that this is a problem that can only be managed, not resolved, and that the costs to U.S. interests throughout the Islamic world from a failure to resolve it can be minimized. The administration may be right about the first assumption but is demonstrably wrong about the second.

How best can one explain President Bush's passivity and willingness to defer constantly to Prime Minister Sharon's preferences in the face of an evolving calamity for U.S. Middle East interests and for the parties to the conflict? The least charitable explanation assumes a unity of thinking between Israel's Likud Party and the Christian Right in the United States limiting the president's options. There is, no doubt, fundamental sympathy in the Bush administration, and indeed among most Americans, for Israel's terrorist dilemma and an unwillingness to ask Israelis to do what we might be unwilling to do in their place.

This said, the Reagan administration acquiesced in Israel's disastrous incursion into Lebanon in 1982, which was led by then General Ariel Sharon. Today, America has become the accomplice in an Israeli approach to the Palestinians, which is both brutal and shortsighted. Sensible Israelis have identified alternative approaches, but these have little chance if the United States remains firmly hitched to Prime Minister Sharon's wagon. On April 14, 2004, in a joint news conference and exchange of letters between President Bush and

Prime Minister Sharon, the merging of Israeli and U.S. policies was announced. The "broker/mediator" role that the United States has played for more than thirty years between Arabs and Israelis is no longer credible. Walter Russell Mead had it right, recently, when he argued that the "United States doesn't need to be less pro-Israel, but we do need to figure out a way to be more pro-Palestinian."[29]

U.S. policymakers will have to confront whether a two-state solution between Palestinians and Israelis is any longer possible. The combination of a Palestinian leadership vacuum and Israeli determination to create facts on the ground may mean that separation of Palestinians and Israelis into two stable and viable states can never be attained. The United States will not impose it, and the parties cannot achieve it. Israel's construction of a West Bank fence will leave a seething mass of Palestinians beyond the fence further alienated by this imposed solution. Israel cannot fence off its problems, which will grow with every Palestinian birth. Israeli leaders must now consider whether their policies will ultimately lead to a decisive rupture of Israel's relations with Egypt and Jordan.

Iran

It is hard to escape the conclusion that U.S. problems with Iran are worsening. Virtually everything that was claimed about Saddam Hussein is true about Iran. There is substantial Iranian support going to terrorist groups, and Iranian officials misled the world about their country's nuclear programs.

Americans must grant that Iran has genuine security concerns. Prior to 9/11, Saddam Hussein, who invaded Iran in 1980, was still in charge in Baghdad, and Afghanistan was controlled by the hostile Taliban. Now both countries are occupied by troops of the Great Satan—the United States. Moreover, Iran has nuclear armed states to its north, west, and east.

Since early 2003, there have been mounting disclosures of the extent of Iran's hidden nuclear program. Iranians argue that Iran can develop a full nuclear fuel cycle and remain party to the Non-Proliferation Treaty. Geoffrey Kemp claims that while Iran is "technically correct . . . it would permit Iran to get all of the ingredients for bomb-making, including enriched uranium and plutonium, but without fabricating a bomb, and then—very suddenly—shift from a civilian research program to a military program with very little notice."[30] Preventing this outcome has engaged members of the European Union, especially Britain, France, Germany and the International Atomic Energy Agency (IAEA). The dilemma is that Iran's nuclear program has broad support in that country among radicals and moderates alike.

It is, of course, not unprecedented for the United States to engage directly with regimes with which it has fundamental disagreements. President Nixon opened a dialogue with the leaders of the People's Republic of China (PRC) when China was actively supporting U.S. enemies in Hanoi and was in the middle of the internal convulsions of the Cultural Revolution.

There exists, however, a sharp split in the U.S. policy community between those favoring initiating a broad dialogue with Iraq's current leaders and those who favor a policy of regime change. The Bush administration seems to have settled for an ambivalent policy somewhere between these extremes but reflective of fissures within the administration. The dilemma remains that Iran has the capacity to do enormous harm to U.S. interests. An Iranian "breakout" from the Non-Proliferation Treaty would inevitably create pressures on Middle East states like Egypt, which have not yet moved to that decision. Moreover, clearly Iran can expand its already significant meddling in Iraq and Afghanistan, to the detriment of U.S. interests.

It remains unclear whether there are the makings of a "grand bargain" whereby Iran would verifiably abandon its efforts to construct a nuclear weapons program, give up its support of Hezbollah and Hamas, and support an Arab-Israeli peace. The United States would, under such a bargain, drop its sanctions on Iran, settle asset claims, and take concrete steps to satisfy Iranian security concerns.

Finding the right balance between carrots and sticks in dealing with Iran will not be easy. However, it is hard to escape the conclusion that current U.S. policies offer few incentives to Iranian leaders to adjust their behavior in the U.S. direction while offering plenty of incentives to harm U.S. interests in the region.

Bush Legacy

> "We are all captives of pictures in our head—our belief that the world we experience is the world that really exists."
>
> Walter Lippman

Later this year, George W. Bush will end his first term. Voters in November will decide whether he will be granted a second term. In the meantime, it is possible to take an initial accounting of his first term foreign policy accomplishments as they relate, in particular, to the Middle East and South Asia.

By any measure, the president has demonstrated that he can and will act decisively. But his policies have raised as many questions as they have answered. A task force assembled by the Stanley Foundation in 2003 issued a report entitled *Strategies for U.S. National Security* that identified "three major ambiguities": "the circumstances in which preventive war and preemptive attacks will be used, the tension between promoting democracy and prosecuting the war on terrorism, and the role of existing alliances versus coalitions of the willing or ad hoc coalitions."[31] These ambiguities have contributed to a widely held international view of the United States as unpredictable and capricious and driven as much by domestic imperatives as by a commitment to building a more stable, safer world.

The American people under President Bush are now back to the type of debate that was common during the Cold War—a debate over means, not ends. There is a national consensus that Islamic terrorism must be confronted, though there is an emerging disconnect between a president who is briefed daily about terrorist threats to the United States and a general populous that seems to feel 9/11 was a unique occurrence.

President Bush reoriented U.S. foreign policy in response to the September 11 attacks, decoupling it from U.S. alliance relationships (in Europe in particular), shifting the country's foreign policy focus to the Middle East and South Asia, and placing primary reliance on military and intelligence operations bolstered by ad hoc coalitions of the willing. He improved relations with large powers—Russia, China, and India in particular. This was in keeping with a strategy that identified rogue states, terrorists, and weapons of mass destruction as posing the greatest risks to the United States. U.S. military victories in Afghanistan and Iraq were decisive and impressive, leaving no question of the U.S.'s mastery of modern war. There can also be little doubt that terrorists and rogue states have received powerful messages about the U.S.'s willingness to use decisive force and take casualties when necessary.

However, the Bush administration has failed to craft effective responses to the political challenges posed by weak states. A number of senior administration officials came to office critical of the very concept of "nation building," dubious about working with the United Nations, and supremely confident in their estimation of the U.S.'s capacity to affect change on its own. Senior civilian leaders in the Department of Defense have shown particular disdain for the views of others. The resulting trench warfare within the administration has contributed to a dysfunctional interagency process and an inability to craft effective U.S. policies on issues ranging from Iraqi and Afghan reconstruction to North Korean negotiations.

On October 22, 2003, a memo from Secretary of Defense Donald Rumsfeld to senior civilian and military officials in the Pentagon leaked to the press. In it, he asked, "Does the U.S. need to fashion a broad, integrated plan to stop the next generation of terrorists? The U.S. is putting relatively little effort into a long-range plan, but we are putting a great deal of effort into trying to stop terrorists. The cost-benefit ratio is against us! Our cost is billions against the terrorists' costs of millions."[32] In this, at least, Secretary Rumsfeld was on the mark.

More broadly, it appears that the United States is in a confrontation with an Islam that has yet to fully define itself. *The Economist*, in a broad survey in September 2003 entitled "In the Name of Islam," suggested that "[A]n optimistic theory holds that violent Islamism reached a peak in the 1980s and 1990s and has now been defeated. The pessimistic theory holds that the Islamists are gaining strength and continue to pose a grave threat to the political order of Muslim states and possibly to the wider world."[33] Much depends on which theory is right.

It is very hard to escape the conclusion that the war in Iraq and U.S. failures to press for an Israeli-Palestinian peace are hurting the war on terrorism. The prime minister of Singapore, a friend of the

United States, said in a May speech, "We are unfortunately now in a situation where Muslim friends of the U.S. feel uncomfortable about speaking out in America's defense and where mainstream Muslims hesitate to condemn extremists lest they be regarded as supporting the West."[34] Why does this matter? "The consensus among security analysts," wrote Tony Karon recently in *Time* "is that the key to eliminating Al-Qaeda as a threat is to transform the permissive political environment which operates in the Muslim world. Instead the opposite has occurred—Muslim anger at the U.S. has reached an all-time high and continues to grow, driven by outrage at U.S. actions in Iraq and Afghanistan and by Israel's actions against the Palestinians."[35]

Too often, the president's rhetoric appears far ahead of the U.S.'s ability or willingness to perform. This has certainly been the case on the issue of Palestinian/Israeli peace. But nowhere is this more true than on the question of democratization in the Middle East. On November 6, 2003, the president proclaimed that "Iraqi democracy will succeed—and that success will send forth the news, from Damascus to Teheran—that freedom can be the future of every nation."[36] Promotion of democracy abroad is part of a proud U.S. tradition supported by Democrats and Republicans alike. But the administration attempts it now at a time of unprecedented dislike of the United States among many or most young Muslims and a skepticism of secular leadership generally in the Arab world. Moreover, all concerned have gotten caught up in the allure of elections in Iraq when, as Steven Erlanger of the *New York Times* rightly notes, "[E]lections by themselves don't translate into parliamentary rule or civilian control or an independent judiciary or fair taxes or protections for private property and minorities."[37] At the end of January 2004, a Lebanese paper, the *Daily Star* (Beirut), editorialized, "But we're also getting slightly worried that the American government may feel that promoting democracy in the Middle East is primarily the responsibility of eloquent speechwriters in Washington, rather than a function of American policies on the ground in the region itself."[38]

The administration pressed forward with its much revised Broader Middle East and North African Initiative officially unveiled at the June 2004 G-8 meeting in Sea Island, Georgia. Ideally, Arab publics and governments will get past the messenger to the message, which emphasizes the need for reform in a region suffering from poor leadership and economic stagnation.

The U.S.'s clearest vulnerability at present is in Iraq, where President Bush has staked his presidency and the U.S.'s credibility. A U.S. failure could come in many forms—from escalating violence to a breakup of the state. At best, U.S. troops and civilians will find it difficult to extricate themselves from the middle of an Iraqi struggle over the future control and shape of their country. Ideally, that struggle will occur in the voting booth as forecast in the June 8, 2004 UN resolution. More likely, it will be waged with guns and bombs. It is hard to escape the conclusion that Bush administration officials were both naïve and uninformed about what to expect in Iraq. Now, if the United States fails, terrorists and fundamentalists throughout the Islamic world will feel emboldened. It is a terrible burden and regrettably an unnecessary one for the United States to bear.

Recent history in the Middle East has demonstrated the power of minorities to block progress. Israeli West Bank and Gaza settlers stand in the way of the desires of the majority of Israelis for a negotiated two state solution to Israel's Palestinian problem. Kurds in Iraq, reflecting a long history of oppression, seek maximum autonomy in a unified state—more autonomy than the majority of Iraqis wish to accord them. Finally, terrorists are undermining the chances of peaceful outcomes from Kashmir to Gaza.

At the heart of the U.S. dilemma—and the Bush legacy—has been the erosion of international relationships—institutional and bilateral. Clearly, on many issues the Bush administration has been prepared to seek cooperative partnerships but, for the most part, these appear to have been constructed of necessity not choice. Only in extremis did the administration turn to the United Nations to assist it out of the morass in Iraq.

Administration spokesmen have regularly emphasized that "the United States will never seek a permission slip to defend the security of our country." To which sentiment Robert Kagan—no enemy of the Bush administration—properly responds, "A nation with global hegemony cannot proclaim to the world that it will be guided only by its own definition of its 'national interest.' That is precisely what even America's closest friends fear: that the United States will wield its vast power only for itself."[39]

In the spring of 2004—with the approach of the November elections—there were signs that the administration was becoming more willing to work with others—in Iraq, on Libya, North Korea, and Iran. Administration flexibility, for example, with respect to the June 8 Security Council resolution on Iraq, was certainly a positive development. What remained unclear was whether these were tactical adjustments or a strategic reorientation. Some conservative observers maintain that we should recognize and adapt to changed circumstances. Charles Krauthammer, for example, argues that "[T]he postwar alliance that once structured and indeed defined our world is dead. It died in 2003."[40]

The risk, of course, is that President Bush's clearest legacy is to demonstrate the limits of U.S. power. The United States knows how to use force but has not yet learned how to translate military victories into political successes. Moreover, winning is sapping the U.S.'s moral strength. Kenneth Pollack argues, "When the United States confronts future challenges, the exaggerated estimates of Iraq's WMD will loom like an ugly shadow over the diplomatic discussions. Fairly or not, no foreigner trusts U.S. intelligence to get it right anymore, or trusts the Bush Administration to tell the truth."[41] The legacy of Abu Ghraib will haunt American policies for years to come.

This diminished trust occurs at a time when financial constraints at home are beginning to kick in and when the president has expanded the U.S. presence and power in the volatile Middle East/ South Asia region farther than at any time in history. The risk, of course, is that should a major crisis spring up elsewhere in the world, the United States will be woefully unprepared to meet it as it struggles to maintain troop levels in Iraq. Candidates for "surprise" include conflict in East Asia or an India-Pakistan eruption, perhaps triggered by a dramatic assassination. The United States, it seems, is poised to experience a classic mismatch between commitments and resources.

Any stragegy for dealing with this mismatch will have to rely on help from allied nations and international organizations. Getting such assistance will require the United States to share responsibilities and decisionmaking in a multinational effort to avoid disasters in the Middle East/South Asian region. The next two chapters look more closely at the prospects for the United States effectively engaging its European and Asian allies and partners in the effort.

Notes

1. George H.W. Bush and Brent Scowcroft, *A World Transformed* (New York, NY: Vintage Books, 1999), 489. (Then Secretary of Defense Dick Cheney said in April 1991, "it would have been a mistake for us to get bogged down in the quagmire inside Iraq.")

2. Robert J. Art, *A Grand Strategy for America* (Ithaca, NY: Cornell University Press, 2003), 9.

3. G. John Ikenberry, *Strategic Reactions to American Preeminence: Great Power Politics in the Age of Unipolarity* (Washington, D.C.: National Intelligence Council [NIC], July 28, 2003), 1.

4. Ibid., 8.

5. Daniel Philpott, "The Challenge of September 11 to Secularism in International Relations," *World Politics* vol. 55, no. 1 (October 2002): 83.

6. Anthony H. Cordesman, "The Strategic Meaning of US Intervention in Iraq: Four Wars and Counting" (Washington, D.C.: Center for Strategic and International Studies, December 1, 2003), 2.

7. Robert I. Rothberg, "Nation-State Failure: A Recurring Phenomenon?" (Washington, D.C.: NIC 2020 Project, November 6, 2003), 2. Pauline Baker, writing at the Fund for Peace, has identified twelve indicators of state collapse, many, but not all of which, apply to Pakistan and some to Saudi Arabia. They are demographic pressures, inadequate provision of public services, factionalized elites, intervention by external political actors, depth of group grievances, uneven development, refugees and displaced persons, human rights, brain drain, sharp economic decline, a security apparatus operating as a "state within a state," and delegitimization of the state.

8. "A Success Worth Noting in Iraq," *New York Times*, February 8, 2004, 14 (editorial).

9. President Clinton, of course, was not the first U.S. leader to fail to craft an effective answer to Middle East terror. Ronald Reagan did no better in Lebanon in the 1980s, when the U.S. embassy and Marine barracks were blown up in quick succession.

10. John R. Bolton, "Should we Take Global Governance Seriously?" *Chicago Journal of International Law* vol. 1, no. 2, (Fall 2000): 221.

11. Condoleezza Rice, "Promoting the National Interest," *Foreign Affairs* (January/February 2000): 53.

12. *The National Security Strategy of the United States of America* (Washington, DC: The White House, September 2002), 6.

13. Ahmed Rashid, "The Mess in Afghanistan," *The New York Review of Books*, February 12, 2004, 25.

14. Nicholas D. Kristof, "Afghan Women, Still in Chains," *New York Times*, February 14, 2004, A29.

15. Raymond Bonner and Don Van Natta Jr., "Regional Terrorist Groups Pose Growing Threat, Experts Warn," *New York Times*, February 8, 2004, 1.

16. Richard Haass, "Wars of Choice," *Washington Post*, November 23, 2003, B7.

17. Charles W. Kegley Jr. and Gregory A. Raymond, "Preventive War and Permissive Normative Order," *International Studies Perspectives* (2003): 388.

18. Kenneth M. Pollack, "Spies, Lies, and Weapons: What Went Wrong," *The Atlantic* vol. 293, no. 1 (January/February 2004): 79.

19. Walter Pucus and Dana Priest, "Bush Aides Ignored CIA Caveats on Iraq," *Washington Post*, February 7, 2004, A17.

20. Quoted in Vincent A. Auger, "Seeking a Simplicity of Statement," *National Security Quarterly* (Spring 1997): 5.

21. Jeffrey Record, "Bounding the Global War on Terrorism" (Washington, D.C.: Army War College, December 2003), V.

22. Quoted in Bill Keller, "The Sunshine Warrior," *New York Times Magazine*, September 22, 2002.

23. Sydney J. Freedberg Jr., "Federalism Can Avert Civil War in Iraq," *National Journal*, February 14, 2004, 475.

24. Pauline Baker, "Iraq as a Failed State: A Six Month Progress Report," *Report #1, Pre-war through September 2003* (Washington, D.C.: The Fund for Peace, 2003), 4.

25. Larry Diamond, *Transition to What?* (Palo Alto, CA: Stanford Institute for International Studies, May 11, 2004), 7.

26. Thomas L. Friedman, "War of Ideas, Part 4," *New York Times*, January 18, 2004.

27. Craig S. Smith, "Israel Says Settlement Population Has Doubled Since '93," *New York Times*, December 31, 2003.

28. Henry Siegman, "Israel: The Threat from Within," *New York Review of Books*, February 26, 2004, 17.

29. Interview with Walter Russell Mead, by Bernard Gwertzman, consulting editor, Council on Foreign Relations, CFA.org, April 9, 2004.

30. Geoffrey Kemp, "U.S. and Iran—The Nuclear Dilemma: Next Steps," (Washington, D.C.: The Nixon Center, April 2004): 13.

31. Laurence Kolb and Michael Kraig, "Strategies for U.S. National Security: Winning the Peace in the 21st Century" (Muscatine, IA: Stanley Foundation, October 2003): 10.

32. Dave Moniz and Tom Squitieri, "Defense Memo: A Grim Outlook," *USA Today*, October 22, 2003, 1.

33. Peter David, "In the Name of Islam," *The Economist*, September 13, 2003, 8.

34. "Beyond Madrid: Winning Against Terrorism," address by Goh ChokTong (prime minister of Singapore) (Washington, D.C.: Council on Foreign Relations, May 6, 2004).

35. Tony Karon, "Why al-Queada Thrives," *Time* online edition, May 27, 2004.

36. "President Bush Discusses Freedom in Iraq and Middle East," remarks by the president at the twentieth anniversary of the National Endowment for Democracy (Washington, D.C.: U.S. Chamber of Commerce, November 6, 2003).

37. Steven Erlanger, "Why Democracy Defies the Urge to Implant It," *New York Times*, February 15, 2004.

38. "Do a Hundred Democratic Deeds Tomorrow," *Daily Star* (Beirut), January 26, 2004.

39. Robert Kagan, "A Decent Regard," *Washington Post*, March 2, 2004, A21.

40. Charles Krauthammer, "A Farewell to Allies: Now They Are Neutrals. America Can Stand Tall Without Them," *Time*, January 12, 2004.

41. Pollack, "Spies, Lies, and Weapons," 92.

3

U.S. Power and Influence in Europe
Stanley R. Sloan

A Valuable Relationship under Stress

The challenges to U.S. foreign policy outlined in the previous chapter require complex responses, including participation of U.S. allies and partners as well as international organizations. The U.S. relationship with Europe could be critical to the questions of how the burdens of maintaining international stability are shared and whether international cooperation and organizations will function in support of U.S. interests.

Since the end of the Cold War, wide gaps have opened up between the United States and its allies in Europe. To some extent, these gaps are the product of structural factors in international relations with which the United States and its allies must deal but that are not easily subject to manipulation. The most important of these is the emergence of the United States as the only global power whose policies and actions inevitably intrude on the sovereign interests of other states, including those of friends and allies.

A related structural factor is that the European allies no longer rely on the United States to defend them against the Soviet Union. Rather, they are partners with the United States in the war against terror, and some of them joined in the U.S.-led coalition that removed Saddam Hussein from power and occupied Iraq. Beyond structural sources of difference, U.S.-European disagreements are the product of choices made in democratic decision-making processes on both sides of the Atlantic, for example concerning resources allocated for

---

*This chapter was prepared with the participation of Robert G. Sutter and Casimir A. Yost.

military systems and operations versus resources made available for other sources of national power and influence.

Since the advent of the Bush administration, European observers and governments have been concerned that U.S. respect for alliances, international law, cooperation, and organizations was being displaced by reliance on overwhelming U.S. military force. Many Europeans saw the United States as abandoning what had been a shared Euro-Atlantic commitment to the rule of law, applied internationally as well as within states.

The U.S.-European relationship has from the early post-World War II period been founded on declarations of common values and interests.[1] Throughout the Cold War, the United States and its allies had differences concerning how best to respond to the Soviet threat. The nature of the threat, however, facilitated resolution of differences and development of common approaches. The new challenges of nonstate terrorist threats and the shadowy relationships between such groups and national governments have yielded a variety of interpretations of the nature of the threat and how best to respond. The September 11, 2001, attacks on the United States produced a sense of joint purpose between the United States and its European allies. But the nature of the U.S. response, particularly with regard to Iraq, has produced serious divisions across the Atlantic and among European states.

Now, as the United States struggles to help establish a democratic regime in Iraq, the question addressed here is whether the behavior of the United States as a hegemonic power has enhanced or diminished its power and influence in Europe and more generally throughout the world.

Why Does it Matter?

For more than fifty years, the United States, Canada, and their European allies have taken the Euro-Atlantic alliance for granted: Maintenance of a strong, vital "transatlantic link" has been at the core of European and U.S. foreign and defense policies. Early in the twenty-first century, however, a new period of questioning has begun. Some Americans ask: If the United States is the world's only superpower, what do weak, disputatious, legalistic Europeans have to offer to U.S. interests? Some Europeans ask: If Europe is on its way to unity, with most European countries on board, why should Europe defer to rude, reckless, impetuous Americans?

The U.S. side of this debate tends to focus on European weakness. Walter Russell Mead, analyzing U.S. perspectives on Europe, has painted a picture of the relationship straight out of a classic U.S. situation comedy, writing,

> When Jacksonian America does think about Europe, it sees what Sheriff Andy of Mayberry saw in Barney Fife—a scrawny, neurotic deputy whose good heart was overshadowed by bad judgment and vanity. The slow-talking, solid Andy tolerated Barney just fine, but he knew that Barney's self-importance would get him into one humiliating scrape after another.[2]

A prominent neoconservative commentator, Robert Kagan, argues that the success of the European integration process, creating a zone of peace and cooperation among countries that had warred for centuries, has also given birth to a "non-use of force ideology." According to Kagan, "This is what many Europeans believe they have to offer the world: not power, but the transcendence of power."[3]

One European commentator says that Kagan is "absolutely right" in judging that "Americans and Europeans no longer share a common 'strategic culture.'" Peter van Ham points out that ". . . for non-Americans, this is gradually becoming a world where the U.S. acts as legislator, policeman, judge and executioner. America sets the rules by its own behaviour, judges others without sticking to these rules itself. . . ."[4]

Such broad caricatures have recently dominated discussion of U.S.-European relations. They lead all too easily to the conclusion that the United States and Europe are drifting apart. There is a factual foundation for such analyses. States tend to use the instruments of statecraft available to them. What instruments they develop and fund are at least somewhat dependent on what their history has taught them. The history of the Second World War led many Europeans to conclude that military conflict is to be avoided at all cost. Meanwhile, many Americans look at World War II as demonstrating that appeasement of dictators only whets their appetite for conquest. During the Cold War, West European nations learned that putting aside old antagonisms allowed them to build a prosperous, stable community—today's European Union. Meanwhile, deterring and finally defeating the Soviet Union in the Cold War reinforced the U.S. conviction that the demonstrated willingness to use force is necessary in dealing with potentially aggressive dictatorial regimes.

There is more to be said, however, about the relevance of U.S.-European relations than such critiques reveal.

First, there is the fact that the United States, Canada, and the members of the European Union share political systems built on the values of democracy, individual liberty, and the rule of law. Granted, this does not mean that these broad values are practiced similarly in all Euro-Atlantic nations. And the fact that they are interpreted differently may help explain the divergent paths chosen for dealing with the Iraq problem. However, the belief in and practice of democracy remain an important part of the foundation for the Euro-Atlantic community.

In addition to shared political values, the United States and EU member states support market-based economic systems in which competition drives the market but is governed by democratically approved rules and regulations. Former Soviet satellites in Central and Eastern Europe and three former Soviet republics (Latvia, Lithuania, and Estonia) have worked hard to adopt "western" political and economic systems. The desire to align with the United States while protecting themselves against excessive Russian influence provided much of the incentive for these unequivocal commitments. They all want to be EU and NATO members to ensure that they are part of Europe and of the Euro-Atlantic community.

Moreover, European and U.S. market economies are the essential core of the global economic system. Along with Japan, the United States and the European Union are the main engines of international trade and investment, and it is therefore in their mutual interest to cooperate to make the system work. The economic relationship between the United States and the European Union is vitally important to both. The European Union is the largest U.S. trade partner when goods and services are added up.[5] The members of the European Union have more than $860 billion of direct investment in the

United States. The United States has some $700 billion invested in EU states. The European Union and the United States together account for more than 40 percent of world trade and represent almost 60 percent of the industrialized world's gross domestic product. These numbers and ratios will continue to grow.[6]

A study by Joseph P. Quinlan has observed that "[W]hen it comes to the bottom line, Europe—by a wide but not fully appreciated margin—remains the most important region of the world for corporate America."[7] Quinlan's study demonstrates that the same is true for corporate Europe and concludes the following:

> In sum, the years since the fall of the Berlin Wall have witnessed one of the greatest periods of transatlantic economic integration in history. Our mutual stake in each other's prosperity has grown dramatically since the end of the Cold War. We ignore these realities at our peril.[8]

At the end of the Cold War, some observers judged that the Soviet threat had imposed a discipline on transatlantic trade and financial relations that would disappear in the post-Cold War era. According to this view, trade differences that had been controlled because of the confrontation with Moscow would break out into the open with a devastating impact on transatlantic relations. Even though the United States and Europe have continued to struggle with a variety of trade issues—most recently including U.S.-imposed tariffs on steel imports and increased subsidies for U.S. farmers—such differences have not shaken the foundations of the relationship. This is so because even though the system stimulates and encourages competition, it also ceases to function effectively unless conflicting interests are eventually reconciled. In spite of continuing differences and the absence of a Cold War threat, the United States and Europe remain committed to resolving their differences in ways that balance costs and benefits over time.

At the heart of the projection of doom and gloom for transatlantic relations by some analysts on both sides of the Atlantic is the view that the U.S.-European security relationship is becoming irrelevant, NATO is dead, and the European Union will never muster enough political will and resources to become a significant military player alongside the United States. There *is* a growing gap between

U.S.- and European-deployed military capabilities. The Europeans have simply not spent enough since the end of the Cold War to keep up with the U.S. revolution in military affairs in which digital technology is being used to revolutionize the modern battlefield. What they have spent has not always been spent well, maintaining military structures and equipment more appropriate for the Cold War strategic environment than for likely twenty-first century conflicts. During the Cold War, the gap between U.S. and European military capabilities produced different preferences for international problem solving. Now, the even-bigger gap yields even more dramatic differences—between the so-called non-use-of-force ideology Robert Kagan ascribes to the Europeans and the unilateral militarism many Europeans see in the Bush administration.

Bush administration Department of Defense political appointees have tended to be skeptical about the willingness of European allies to make serious defense improvements. Granted, the European military modernization picture is certainly bad, but it is not hopeless. Europe clearly needs to invest much more in defense, but the major European military establishments are trying to develop the capacity to conduct future operations on the kind of high-tech battlefield that U.S. capabilities have created. Scheduled improvements in communications, intelligence, surveillance, and reconnaissance; all-weather precision weaponry; strategic mobility; and force projection during the next fifteen years, if carried out, should produce European forces that are more capable of conducting operations in a great variety of battlefield conditions in coalition with the United States and, to a lesser extent, on their own if necessary.[9] The question, of course, is whether political leaders will back up such plans with the required resources.

The debate over Iraq highlighted U.S. differences with some of its key European allies. This did not change the fact that Europe remains the prime source of allies that are willing and able to deploy substantial military forces in zones of conflict far from their borders.[10] Moreover, the main framework for coordinating U.S.-European military cooperation, NATO, has become an important instrument for international, not just European, peace and security. This process took dramatic steps forward, even in the heat of the debate over Iraq, as the NATO allies—including opponents of U.S.

Iraq policy France and Germany—agreed to give NATO a command role in Afghanistan and to support the Polish command in Iraq. Moreover, also during this period of stress, the allies agreed to create a NATO Response Force, composed mainly of European troops and equipment, designed to deploy quickly with modern, effective forces to deal with future military crises—in or beyond Europe.

The European Union and its member states can bring together a rich package of assets required for crisis management and avoidance, including diplomatic mediation, peacekeeping forces, police forces, humanitarian assistance, and development aid. As one U.S.-European expert study group concluded, "Although the U.S. may be able to win wars without significant allied contributions, it is unlikely in many situations to be able to win the peace without military (and non-military) assistance from European allies, whether those situations develop within or outside Europe."[11]

Productive functioning of the international economic system depends on U.S.-European collaboration. International security problems are most easily and effectively handled when the United States and its European allies work together. NATO is a unique instrument for coordination of U.S. and European military forces that could be even more important in a continuing struggle against terrorism. To the extent that the UN Security Council remains an important instrument for international stability and, in Washington, for the pursuit of U.S. policy objectives, the roles of Britain, France, and Russia as permanent, veto-holding members of the council remain critical. The question is how well the United States has been managing this fundamental building block for the U.S. role in the world.

Post-Cold War U.S. Foreign Policy Seen from Europe

Since the end of the Cold War, European perceptions of the United States have swung from concern about the United States drawing inward and abandoning international activism, to fear of a higher U.S. priority on Asian than European relationships, to more recent worries about U.S. unilateralism and hegemonic behavior. The debate in the United States on its post-Cold War role in the world and U.S. actions suggesting one or another outcome has stimulated these varied European perceptions. Perhaps because of the closeness of the ties across the Atlantic, even ripples in U.S. foreign policy sometimes produce tidal waves on European shores.

Since the Cold War ended, there has been an ongoing elite debate about the role the United States should play in an international system that is no longer dominated by the bipolar confrontation of two alliance systems led by the United States and the Soviet Union.

President George Bush (the forty-first president) clearly believed that the United States was required to play a strong international leadership role. Some of his advisers, including some who are senior officials in the George W. Bush (the forty-third president) administration, apparently thought the United States should use its position as the sole superpower to discourage challenges to that position, even among current allies. George Bush (forty-first president) nonetheless accepted the importance of building consensus in the United Nations and constructing coalitions to deal with international challenges (both illustrated by his orchestration of the response to Iraq's invasion of Kuwait). Europeans largely appreciated the respect for international cooperation and organizations deployed by the Bush (forty-first president) administration and its efforts to build a substantial international coalition with UN backing to push Saddam Hussein's forces out of Kuwait.

In the first year of his presidency, Bill Clinton and his foreign policy advisers experimented with a number of different approaches to U.S. foreign policy. President Clinton sought to convert his successful campaign slogan, "It's the economy, stupid," into a pillar of U.S. foreign policy. In part as a consequence of this philosophy, some Clinton administration officials argued that Asia (rather than Europe) should be the central focus of U.S. foreign policy because of the opportunities presented by growing Asian markets. The suggestion that the Clinton administration would try to play Asia off against Europe to promote U.S. trade and economic interests worried Europeans. By the end of 1993, however, the administration had moved to a posture emphasizing continuing U.S. political, economic, and strategic interests in Asia *and* Europe.

For most of President Clinton's first term, the administration seemed to shift between active internationalism and foreign policy reticence. The mood in the country toward foreign entanglements was soured by the peacekeeping disaster in Somalia in 1993. The administration was reluctant to get U.S. troops involved in Yugoslavia, and there was a tendency more broadly toward self-deterrence—conscious avoidance of international involvements that might cost U.S. lives and money.[12] This gave rise to European concerns that the United States might move in isolationist directions. But, in 1996, as he campaigned for a second term in office, President Clinton argued that the United States was the world's "indispensable power," suggesting that the international system required the active involvement of the United States to function effectively. Clinton maintained that such activism was in the U.S. interest and the United States took the lead in attempting to bring peace to the Balkans. European allies greatly appreciated this sign of U.S. interest in stabilizing international crisis zones, particularly in Europe, even if they were not always comfortable with the U.S. lead.

The more assertive U.S. approach also generated European concerns about growing "unilateralist" tendencies in U.S. policy. Even though overall foreign policy was seen as supporting multilateral approaches, Europeans identified several early signs of U.S. unilateralism and hegemonic tendencies, including

◆ the "Helms-Burton Act" that sought to impose sanctions on non-U.S. firms doing business with Cuba;

◆ congressional insistence on reform of the United Nations as a precondition for payment of U.S. arrears;

◆ hard-line sanctions toward Iran, Iraq, and Libya;

◆ refusal in the mid-1990s to give up NATO's Southern Command to a European officer;

◆ the Clinton administration's approach to the June 1997 Denver economic summit, which was seen by some participants as "in your face" bragging about the success of the U.S. economic model (at which leaders were asked to put on cowboy hats and boots for the group picture);

◆ Clinton insistence on limiting the first group of candidates for NATO membership to three countries, when several European countries favored a larger group;

◆ U.S. refusal to sign the treaty banning antipersonnel land mines; and

◆ U.S. proposals in 1998 that NATO should be able to use force even when it is not possible to obtain a mandate from the UN Security Council.

Critics in Europe and elsewhere suggested the United States was beginning to act like a classic, overbearing hegemonic power, using its position of supremacy in the international system to have its way at the expense of the interests and preferences of other powers. Russia complained about NATO enlargement, and China advocated a "multipolar" world as an alternative to U.S. hegemony. In April 1997, Boris Yeltsin and Chinese leader Jiang Zemin agreed on a "strategic partnership" against those who would "push the world toward a unipolar order." European allies occasionally joined the critique overtly. In December 1998, chairman of the Defense Committee in the French National Assembly Socialist Paul Quiles warned that NATO's fiftieth anniversary summit in Washington in April 1999 should not "set the seal on the United States' hegemony over the alliance."

In this same period, at least one European observer argued that U.S. hegemonic tendencies were different and less dangerous than those of previous hegemons. This circumstance, Josef Joffe argued, could not be seen simply in classic balance-of-power terms. He argued the United States was different from previous dominant powers: "It irks and domineers, but it does not conquer. It tries to call the shots and bend the rules, but it does not go to war for land and glory."13 Further, he suggested, the dominating U.S. position is based on "soft" as well as "hard" power: "This type of power—a culture that radiates outward and a market that draws inward—rests on pull, not on push; on acceptance, not on conquest."14

The George W. Bush (forty-third president) administration therefore came to office in 2001 facing a mix of European fears and expectations. Candidate Bush had made statements suggesting the United States should begin to pull back from some of its overseas commitments, but the overall thrust of administration policy was in unilateralist directions, at least as most Europeans saw it.

The first foreign policy actions of the Bush administration tended to raise warning flags for European governments. Unilateral U.S. decisions not to join in the International Criminal Court, to remain outside the Kyoto Protocol on greenhouse gas emissions, and to terminate the Anti-Ballistic Missile Treaty with Russia were all seen as signs that the United States was heading in new directions based almost exclusively on short-term U.S. policy choices and with no regard for their impact on the views or interests of its closest allies.

The 9/11 Shock

When terrorists mounted the September 11, 2001 attacks against U.S. targets, the European allies responded with unqualified sympathy and support in spite of their ongoing concerns about U.S. foreign policy directions. This included understanding and offers of support for U.S. operations in Afghanistan to remove the Taliban government from power and destroy the Al-Qaeda terrorist network that had established itself under Taliban protection. However, the Bush administration was slow to respond to many of the offers of assistance and, from a European point of view, appeared to be sending the message that the United States did not appreciate or need the assistance offered. The administration's assertion that "the mission should determine the coalition" raised questions about whether the administration was downgrading NATO as an instrument for U.S.-European military cooperation.

In addition, most Americans saw the 9/11 attacks as producing a fundamental change in the international environment. Led by the Bush administration, a war mentality became the core of the U.S.'s world view. Many Europeans, on the other hand, saw the attacks as part of a continuing struggle with terrorism rather than a new phase of international relations. They tended to focus on the need to deal with the causes of Islamic fundamentalist terrorism as aggressively as the United States was dealing with its consequences. These post-9/11 disconnects between Europe and the United States were signs of a bigger problem to come, as the Bush administration focused its attention on Iraq as the next target.

The Iraq Factor

The Bush administration's approach to Iraq produced serious divisions between the United States and some of its key European allies as well as within Europe itself. No European government saw Saddam Hussein and his regime as benign, and all agreed that something more serious needed to be done to replace sanctions that had hurt the Iraqi people more than the Hussein regime. But there were differences about whether Iraq possessed weapons of mass destruction, the links between Hussein's regime and Al-Qaeda, and the imminence of the threat posed by Iraq.

Early in 2002, it was clear to many European observers that the Bush administration was planning on removing Saddam Hussein from office, with force if necessary, and with or without the support of the international community.[15] This enhanced the sense among many Europeans that the United States had taken on an "arrogance of power" that was inconsistent with both traditional U.S. foreign policy and the basis of U.S.-European alliance and cooperation.

By the time the Bush administration, at the urging of Bush's close ally British Prime Minister Tony Blair, finally decided to take its case to the United Nations in September 2002, few Europeans believed that the approach was intended to find a peaceful resolution of the Iraq problem. Vice President Cheney in a major speech in August had made it quite clear that the administration believed Hussein would have to be removed by force.[16]

Many Europeans suspected that the approach to the UN Security Council was primarily designed to serve domestic political purposes, secondarily to firm up Tony Blair's support, and only incidentally to get UN Security Council approval. Public opinion polls late in the summer of 2002 had shown that the American people favored going to war against Iraq only if the United States were supported by the international community. With the midterm election campaigns underway, and control of the Congress potentially in the balance, some Europeans thought the administration was simply protecting its electoral flanks. This suspicion was reinforced by comments made by the president's political adviser, Karl Rove, suggesting that the approach to the United Nations was in fact desirable for domestic political purposes.[17]

In the end, Blair's insistence that the UN string be run out prolonged the attempt to get UN approval for an attack on Iraq. However, very few Europeans were convinced that the Bush administration had any intention of suspending its plans to attack, particularly given the massive military buildup around Iraq that had begun late in 2002. Some European governments sympathized with the need to remove Hussein from power, but many thought all other options should be tested before resorting to the use of force.

Early in 2003, the issue of whether to begin planning defensive assistance to Turkey should it be attacked by Iraq during a presumptive U.S.-led coalition attack on Saddam Hussein's regime exploded, threatening the very underpinnings of the alliance. On January 15, U.S. Deputy Secretary of Defense Paul Wolfowitz formally asked NATO to consider what supporting roles it might play in a U.S.-led war on Iraq. Six areas of assistance were discussed, including sending Patriot missiles and AWACS surveillance planes to defend Turkey, the only NATO member that borders Iraq.

After considerable discussion within the North Atlantic Council, Belgium, France, and Germany publicly announced their opposition to allowing NATO to begin planning to provide military assistance to Turkey. The three recalcitrant allies said they were not opposed to aiding Istanbul but believed that planning for such action was premature while UN arms inspectors were still seeking to disarm Iraq peacefully. The initiative was seen as an attempt by the United States to get preemptive NATO support for a military action that was not sanctioned by the UN Security Council. Once before, in the case of Kosovo, NATO had acted without a Security Council mandate. In that case, however, all the allies agreed that Russia and China should not be allowed to block a military action in Europe deemed necessary by the NATO allies. In this case, the three allies wanted to make it clear that a NATO mandate would not be sufficient to justify military action against Iraq. The choices of the United States to put the issue before the alliance and of the three allies to block the requested planning brought existing political differences over Iraq into NATO in a form that put NATO's mutual defense commitment on the line.

To break the stalemate, NATO Secretary General Robertson and some member states suggested taking the issue to the Defense Planning Committee (DPC), in which France still chooses not to participate. Agreement was finally reached in the French-less DPC when Belgium and Germany dropped their opposition to beginning planning possible military aid to Turkey.

The scenario illustrated to what extent the Iraq issue had frayed political bonds among the allies. It also demonstrated that NATO remains an alliance of sovereign states and that it works only when serious efforts have been made to build a political consensus behind a course of action, particularly when that action requires the use of military force.

The Bush administration worked hard to get as many European governments as possible on board in support of the war. In addition to the Blair government, the most responsive European governments were those that had been liberated from Soviet control by the successful end of the Cold War. For many of these countries, the goal of eliminating one of the world's most despotic dictators undoubtedly seemed more compelling than for those countries that for decades had experienced peace, democracy, and financial well-being.[18] The list of European countries that supported the war effort in principle was substantial.[19] The United Kingdom contributed combat troops and played a significant role in the attack on Iraq and in the postwar occupation. Poland took charge of a postwar military region in Iraq and Spain and Italy contributed paramilitary and intelligence units. Even in countries whose governments supported the war, however, public opinion remained strongly critical.

The initial war against Hussein's regime in Iraq was militarily successful, resulting in the overthrow of Hussein and the eventual capture of the former leader and elimination or capture of most of his top lieutenants. But Europeans remained unconvinced. In the summer of 2003, when asked "was the war in Iraq worth the loss of life and other costs," 70 percent of all Europeans polled answered "no," while only 25 percent said "yes." Even in the states whose governments supported the war, the results were negative. In states whose government supported the war effort, majorities answered in the negative including: the United Kingdom (55 percent); Poland (67 percent); Italy (73 percent); Portugal (75 percent); and the Netherlands (59 percent). In the two leading European opponents of the war, the results were even more emphatic: France (87 percent) and Germany (85 percent).[20]

An in-depth analysis of the European public following the Iraq war came to the conclusion that opposition to the war was at least partly rooted in the perception that the United States was acting unilaterally and without reference to international opinion. According to this analysis, ". . . it makes a significant difference whether a potential military action involved a unilateral U.S. move or one supported by NATO or the U.N. In Europe support increases from 36% for the U.S. acting alone to 48% for an action under a U.N. mandate."[21]

Following the Iraq war, one influential European commentator who had earlier defended the U.S. role as a benign hegemon cautioned the Bush administration and other Americans not to sacrifice the goodwill and cooperation that had for decades constituted part of the foundation for American power. Pro-American commentator Josef Joffe responded to the growing U.S. unilateralist tendencies by observing that the United States would remain the dominant force in international affairs for some time to come and that no traditional power balance would be provided by another power or combination of powers. However, in Joffe's view, U.S. self-interests would not be well served by a strategy based on a "with us or against us" philosophy like that deployed by President Bush following the 9/11 attacks. Rather, according to Joffe, the United States should assume the inevitable costs that are associated with international leadership.

> Primacy does not come cheap, and the price is measured not just in dollars and cents, but above all in the currency of obligation. Conductors manage to mold 80 solo players into a symphony orchestra because they have a fine sense for everybody else's quirks and qualities—because they act in the interest of all; their labour is the source of their authority. . . . Power exacts responsibility, and responsibility requires the transcendence of narrow self-interest. As long as the United States continues to provide such public goods, envy and resentment will not escalate into fear and loathing that spawn hostile coalitions.[22]

Late in 2003, when it had appeared the Bush administration was attempting to broaden the base of international support for Iraqi stabilization and reconstruction, and just before George Bush was scheduled to call the leaders of Germany, France, and Russia to ask them to forgive old Iraqi debt, the administration took another unilateral step that surprised and angered the European governments that had opposed the war. A directive from Deputy Secretary of Defense Paul Wolfowitz—cleared by the White House—was posted on the Pentagon Web site making it clear that only Iraq coalition members would be eligible to serve as prime contractors for U.S.-financed reconstruction projects in Iraq. This eliminated three key countries Bush was about to ask for Iraqi debt relief and others, including Canada. The predictable reaction was immediate. German foreign minister Joschka Fischer said that the move would "not be acceptable" to Germany, "and it wouldn't be in line with the spirit of looking to the future together and not into the past."[23] The move undermined the diplomatic efforts of Secretary of State Powell to build international support for Iraqi debt relief. Russian Defense Minister Sergei Ivanov spoke out in opposition to forgiveness of Iraq's $120 billion debt, $8 billion of which is owed to Russia. Ivanov noted "Iraq is not a poor country."[24]

Just prior to release of the contracting decision, former Secretary of State James Baker had been asked to travel to Europe to convince key allied states to forgive Iraqi debt as a contribution to Iraqi recovery from the war. Baker received a cool reception in Paris, Berlin, and Moscow, but the three key governments all agreed to negotiate some package of debt reductions. Irritated by the U.S. contracting decision, French President Chirac, German Chancellor Schroeder, and Russian President Putin all decided to handle the debt reduction issue via normal diplomatic channels, which in this case would be through the "Paris Club," a group of nineteen industrialized nations that have collaborated since 1956 on easing financial burdens of heavily indebted nations.[25]

Consequences: How Do Perceptions Affect Policies, Actions, Attitudes and U.S. Interests?

U.S. hegemony after 1945 was viewed in Europe as benevolent in the sense that Washington decided to cooperate with its allies rather than dominating them, that it agreed to tame its power by being locked into multilateral organizations, and that its political system was open to access by its allies thus offering them the opportunity to influence U.S. decision-making.[26] As a result, Washington's leadership had to do with (hard and soft) power but did not solely rest on it. Leadership is an interactive process where the leader is followed because he is able to convince the followers. By taking into account the needs and goals of its allies and by listening to and caring about their opinion, the United States managed to base followership on persuasion and normative consensus, or soft power.[27] When the leader neglects to bring its soft power into play in support of military actions, however, would-be followers find the first occasion to deviate. This is exactly what has happened in recent years and what led to the transatlantic crisis over Iraq.

Unilateralism—whether in the hard-nosed form deployed by the current Bush administration or in the more occasional, cushioned, and velvet form of the former Clinton administration—is seen from Europe a clear sign of a shifting balance between reliance on hard and soft power in U.S. foreign policy. It provokes criticism because it puts at risk the international normative consensus and undermines the institutional framework.[28] Before September 11 and certainly afterwards, the new Bush administration interpreted U.S. sovereignty as nonnegotiable, thus refuting international commitments that might limit the administration's leeway or force it to seek the consensus of others where independent actions would be preferred. In the long run, however, this tendency undermines the attractiveness of the U.S. political, cultural, and societal model, thereby threatening the core of U.S. soft power.

International public opinion polls conducted in the aftermath of the war on Iraq clearly underlined this danger. According to a study conducted by the Pew Research Center, the rate of those people that somewhat or very much disapprove of the United States increased markedly in Italy, whose government supported the war, (38 percent in May 2003 vs. 23 percent in summer 2002), in France (57 percent vs. 34 percent), and Germany (54 percent vs. 35 percent). The same study also highlighted a growing preparedness of these countries' populations to loosen the NATO ties to the United States. The most extreme shift was seen in U.S.-ally Turkey, where more than 80 percent (vs. 55 percent in summer 2002) have an unfavorable opinion of the United States.[29] Extensive public opinion polling in the early months of 2004 revealed even stronger European public skepticism about the war against Iraq and questioning of U.S. leadership.[30]

The foundation for and history of U.S.-European relations since World War II may help explain the intensity of European feeling concerning U.S. unilateral behavior. The transatlantic alliance has always been based on common interests, to be sure. But behind any cold, hard assessment of national interests, this relationship has always been fortified and defended by a sense of common values. Europeans, not possessing the same degree of military power and superpower status as the United States, still believe that they are as responsible as is the United States for defining and defending the common values that countries on both sides of the Atlantic say they share. From a European point of view, the United States has recently strayed from a shared appreciation of international cooperation, institutions, and the rule of law. In some respects, the Bush administration appeared to be declaring a new global corollary to the Monroe Doctrine, essentially claiming the U.S. right to intervene anywhere in the world to correct wrongdoing as perceived by the United States.[31] From this perspective, Europeans see themselves as defending the foundations of the transatlantic relations that U.S. actions have undermined.

The widespread European perception of U.S. unilateralist and hegemonic behavior has not resulted in any formal alliance or conspiracy to balance U.S. influence. It has, however, increased tendencies toward cooperation among European countries in cases where U.S. policy choices run contrary to perceived interests of two or more European states.

The most dramatic case of this situation to date was the collaboration between France and Germany (with a few other European countries, Belgium, for example, on the margins) to complicate implementation of the U.S. policy of attacking Iraq and removing Saddam Hussein from power. Prior to this case, U.S. rejection of the Kyoto Protocol on international environmental standards resulted in all members of the European Union joining together to criticize the U.S. position.

Perhaps the most important impact on European policies and actions has been more subtle. U.S. policy preferences and initiatives are not judged simply on their merits but also on whether the U.S.

approach is a unilateral one or one designed to attract broad European and international support. Such questioning clearly contributed to the widespread reticence in the international community to provide active assistance to the United States in overthrowing Saddam Hussein's regime with military force and then stabilizing and reconstructing post-Saddam Iraq. Even though the Bush administration can claim success in convincing many European states to join in both the war and the reconstruction effort, the absence of three important states (France, Germany, and Russia) from the coalition can be seen as at least partly attributable to U.S. unilateralism. It is difficult to separate out the role of perceived U.S. unilateralism from disagreement with the U.S. policy in the behavior of these states. It is somewhat clearer, however, that the approach taken by the United States to the question of whether/when to go to war against Iraq influenced the willingness of these governments to participate actively in the stabilization and reconstruction process.

It can also be argued that U.S. unilateralism played a role in the attempt to convince France, Germany, and Russia to make substantial contributions to the process of forgiving Iraqi debt. Although all three eventually decided to help out, their participation has not been as generous as the United States would have liked. The reticence of these important players in the Iraqi debt forgiveness process can arguably be linked to their displeasure with the way in which the United States went to war and the preemptive exclusion of companies from noncoalition partners from the bidding process for prime contracts for Iraqi reconstruction.

The March 2004 defeat of the conservative government in Spain was widely interpreted in Europe as a vote against the government's close ties to the Bush administration and its policies. Very few Europeans shared the view of some Americans that the March 11 terrorist bombing of commuter trains in Madrid just prior to the elections had revealed the cowardice of Spaniards and Europeans more generally. In any case, the ouster of the Spanish government constituted the first clear "cost" to the United States of its perceived unilateralism. With the new Socialist government's promise to pull Spanish troops out of Iraq as soon as possible, the U.S. goals of broadening international involvement in the long-term process of stabilizing and reconstructing the country have been seriously damaged.

The Outlook

Looking ahead, a continued pattern of perceived or actual U.S. unilateralism could produce significant costs for U.S. foreign policy. The long-established democratic governments in Western Europe all carry forward a strong commitment to the values on which international cooperation, law, and organization have been based since the Second World War. Many of these governments and peoples instinctively feel that the system is not owned just by the United States. They believe their democracies played a role in creating and sustaining the system. When the United States attempts to change underlying aspects of that system, and particularly when the U.S. government attempts to do so unilaterally based on overwhelming U.S. power, they are inclined to question and perhaps even oppose such U.S. efforts. This factor will remain an important influence on the way in which European democracies respond to U.S. policy priorities and goals.

European governments do not wish to see the United States "fail" in Iraq, as they too would suffer the consequences of a U.S. defeat there. However, many governments would undoubtedly like the United States to come away from the Iraq experience humbled by the difficulties of accomplishing security objectives without a broad, supportive international coalition. They would like the United States to pay more attention to European policy preferences in the Middle Eastern region (for example by adopting a more balanced stance regarding the Israeli/Palestinian conflict) and to pursue multilateral versus unilateral approaches to both Middle Eastern issues and the war on terror.

No U.S. allies in Europe are likely to turn actively against the United States. France, traditionally the most severe European critic of U.S. policy, supports continued U.S.-European and U.S.-French cooperation, even if Paris would prefer to shift the balance between overwhelming-U.S. and more limited-French influence over international developments. All European governments still feel strong bonds to the United States, ranging from shared fundamental values and basic interests to pragmatic considerations.

All the important states in Europe are democracies (with an appropriate footnote reflecting the qualified nature of Russian democracy), however. The pattern of public opinion established by the Iraq affair can be reversed with changed U.S. behavior. But if it should continue, even the governments most friendly to the United States will find it increasingly difficult to support U.S. policy objectives. If the United States cannot convince more countries to join in the process of stabilizing and reconstructing Iraq—or even convince current members of the coalition to remain engaged—the United States will pay a significant long-term price in lives and national treasure trying to accomplish the task with limited international assistance.

The widespread public disapproval of U.S. policies did not keep several European governments from supporting U.S. policies toward Iraq and joining the U.S.-led coalition. But if the United States continues to be seen by majorities in most European countries as an overbearing, hegemonic power, it will be increasingly difficult for European political parties to take positions that are openly warm and friendly toward the United States. European governments may go along with U.S. initiatives because they serve European interests or because U.S. power is so overwhelming that they have no choice. There will likely be a marked reticence to be too closely identified with the United States and its policies, however, if such identification is likely to diminish popular support at the next election. Over time, the United States could find it increasingly difficult to line up support behind its policies.

In particular, the United States could pay a large price in its relationship with the United Kingdom for Prime Minister Tony Blair's strong support for U.S. policy on Iraq. The widespread opinion in the United Kingdom is that Blair's alignment with Bush accomplished nothing for the United Kingdom and, in fact, undermined British interests in the Middle East, in the struggle against terrorism, and in Europe. This perception could lead Blair and future British leaders to be more reluctant than in the past to support controversial U.S. positions and could produce more British coalitions with its EU partners to shape alternatives to such U.S. approaches.

Such a long-term shift in public and governmental attitudes could seriously undermine U.S. "soft power" foreign policy resources. At a time when the military power of the United States remains superior to that of any other country or group of countries, U.S. influence could decline, particularly in circumstances where it has to rely on the trust and cooperation of other governments. On the other hand, a return to more traditional U.S. foreign policy behavior that includes a mix of multilateral cooperation and unilateral actions when necessary as well as a balanced blend of hard and soft power would undoubtedly begin to mitigate current European concerns about the U.S. role in the world.

At a time when the American people feel under imminent threat from terrorist attacks, the president can say, as President Bush did in his January 2004 State of the Union address, that the United States does not need a "permission slip" from anybody to defend itself. This remains true, even in "normal" times. However, the American people do not want their government to be the world's only policeman. U.S. public opinion surveys for more than a decade have demonstrated that the vast majority of Americans believe the United States should help maintain international peace but should share such burdens and responsibilities with friends and allies. Meeting this public opinion demand over the long term will require U.S. policies and actions that attract support and involvement from key U.S. allies in Europe and around the globe.

Notes

1. Including, most notably, the 1949 North Atlantic Treaty establishing the North Atlantic Treaty Organization (NATO).

2. Walter Russell Mead, "The Case Against Europe," *Atlantic Monthly*, April 2002.

3. Robert Kagan, "Power and Weakness," *Policy Review* (June-July 2002).

4. Peter van Ham in Stanley Sloan and Peter van Ham, *What future for NATO?* (London: Centre for European Reform, October 2002).

5. Canada is the largest single merchandise trading partner for the United States (excluding services from the calculation).

6. For updated figures, see "EU/U.S. Facts and Figures," (Washington, D.C., Delegation of the European Commission to the United States). Available at http://www.eurunion.org/profile/facts.htm (last accessed January 6, 2004).

7. Joseph P. Quinlan, "Drifting Apart or Growing Together? The primacy of the Transatlantic Economy" (Washington, D.C., Center for Transatlantic Relations, 2003).

8. Ibid., 11.

9. See U.S.-CREST, *Future Military Coalitions: The Transatlantic Challenge* (Arlington, VA: September 2002). (This nongovernmental, four nation [France, Great Britain, Germany and the United States] project examined how the development of a common European security and defense policy might affect the conduct of transatlantic coalition operations during the next fifteen years. The author was a core participant in the project and contributor to the final report.) See also Robert P. Grant and Stanley R. Sloan, "Don't Write Off the Allies," *Defense News*, March 25–31, 2002.

10. Some Asian allies, Australia, South Korea and Japan most notably, are capable of contributing forces to international operations and have done so, most recently in Iraq. But potential European contributions are magnified by the willingness and ability of British and French forces to engage in operations far from their borders and the integrating military framework provided by NATO that enhances the value of contributions by other European countries.

11. U.S.-CREST, *Future Military Coalitions.*

12. Stanley R. Sloan, "The United States and the Use of Force in the Post-Cold War World: Away from Self-Deterrence?" Congressional Research Service Report 97–78 F (Washington, D.C.: The Library of Congress, Congressional Research Service, January 6, 1997).

13. Josef Joffe, "How America Does It," *Foreign Affairs* (September/October 1997): 16.

14. Ibid., 24.

15. The discussion of European perceptions that follows is based on extensive conversations with European diplomats, scholars, and citizens during the course of 2002 as well as surveys of the popular press and public opinion poll data.

16. Vice President Richard Cheney, remarks by the vice president to the Veterans of Foreign Wars, 103rd National Convention, August 26, 2002. (See the speech text at http://www.whitehouse.gov/news/releases/2002/08/20020826.html (last accessed January 7, 2004).) This speech, making a strong call for removing Saddam Hussein for power, is frequently cited by German observers as having been the final straw forcing German Chancellor Schroeder to take a strong position against attacking Iraq in the final stages of his reelection campaign.

17. For an example of this perception, see Dan Plesch, "Why war is now on the back burner," *Guardian* (London). Available at http://www.guardian.co.uk/usa/story/0,12271,853427,00.html (last accessed January 7, 2004).)

18. The White House even noted in April 2003 ". . . it is no accident that many member nations of the Coalition recently escaped from the boot of a tyrant or have felt the scourge of terrorism. All Coalition member nations understand the threat Saddam Hussein's weapons pose to the world and the

devastation his regime has wreaked on the Iraqi people." Source: http://
www.whitehouse.gov/infocus/iraq/news/2003032710.html (last accessed on
January 6, 2004).

19. On April 3, 2003, almost two weeks after the opening of hostilities
in Iraq, the White House listed some forty-nine Coalition members, including
the following twenty-three European (including former Soviet republics)
states: Albania, Azerbaijan, Bulgaria, Czech Republic, Denmark, Estonia,
Georgia, Hungary, Iceland, Italy, Latvia, Lithuania, Macedonia, the Netherlands, Poland, Portugal, Romania, Slovakia, Spain, Turkey, Ukraine, United
Kingdom, and Uzbekistan.

20. Data quoted are from Ronald Asmus, Philip P. Everts, and
Pierangelo Isernia, "Power, War and Public Opinion: Thoughts on the Nature
and Structure of the Trans-Atlantic Divide," *Transatlantic Trends 2003*, a
project of the German Marshal Fund of the United States and the Compagnia
di San Paolo. Available at http://www.transatlantictrends.org/ (last accessed
January 6, 2004).)

21. Ibid., 12.

22. Josef Joffe, "Gulliver Unbound: Can America Rule the World?" the
Twentieth Annual John Bonython Lecture (Sydney, Australia: The Centre for
Independent Studies, August 5, 2003). Available at http://www.cis.org.au/
Events/JBL/JBL03.htm (last accessed January 6, 2004).)

23. Erin E. Arvedlund, "Allies Angered at Exclusion From Bidding,"
http://www.nytimes.com, December 11, 2003.

24. Ibid.

25. Craig S. Smith, "France Gives Baker Lukewarm Commitment on
Iraqi Debt," nytimes.com, December 16, 2003.

26. John Gerard Ruggie, "Multilateralism: The Anatomy of an Institu-
tion," in *Multilateralism Matters: The Theory and Praxis of an Institutional
Form*, ed. John Gerard Ruggie (New York: Columbia University Press,
1993), 3–47; Peter F. Cowhey, "Elect Locally-Order Globally. Domestic Politics and Multilateral Cooperation," in Ruggie, *Multilateralism Matters*, 157–
200; G. John Ikenberry, *After Victory: Institutions, Strategic Restraint, and
the Rebuilding of Order After Major Wars* (Princeton: Princeton University
Press, 2001); Thomas Risse-Kappen, *Cooperation among Democracies. The
European Influence on U.S. Foreign Policy* (Princeton: Princeton University
Press, 1995).

27. James MacGregor Burns, *Leadership* (New York: Harper & Row,
1997).

28. John Gerard Ruggie, "Embedded liberalism and the postwar economic regimes," in *Constructing the World Polity. Essays on International
Institutionalization*, ed. John Gerard Ruggie (London, New York: Routledge,
1998), 62–84.

29. Meg Bortin, "In war's wake, hostility and mistrust," *International
Herald Tribune*, June 4, 2003, 1, 6. The report, "Views of a Changing World

2003," is available at http://people-press.org/reports/display.php3?ReportID=185 (accessed December 12, 2003)).

30. Susan Sacs, "Poll Finds Hostility Hardening Toward U.S. Policies," *New York Times*, March 17, 2004.

31. The original Monroe Doctrine (1823) was aimed at keeping European powers out of Latin America. President Theodore Roosevelt's "corollary" to the doctrine, articulated in his annual message to Congress in December 1904, declared that ". . . in the Western Hemisphere the adherence of the United States to the Monroe Doctrine may force the United States, however reluctantly, in flagrant cases of such wrongdoing [terrorism in today's context] or impotence [failed states in today's context], to the exercise of an international police power." (Thanks to Helmut Sonnenfeldt for calling attention to the fact that the Europeans like the Bush policy no better than they liked the Monroe Doctrine or its corollary.)

4

U.S. Power and Influence in Asia

ROBERT G. SUTTER

Summary

Bush administration unilateralism over Iraq and other issues has been widely perceived and criticized among Asian popular and elite opinion, but it is a secondary consideration to most Asian governments. The latter are focused on domestic concerns involving conventional nation building, and they remain wary of one another as they deal with immediate and dangerous security issues in Asia. Asian governments also give much higher priority to dangerous crises in East Asia, particularly North Korea, than to Iraq or U.S. unilateralism elsewhere. They find that over the past two years the Bush administration has behaved in a consultative and moderate way on North Korea, reassuring Asian powers. For these kinds of reasons, Asian governments generally have reacted more pragmatically to Bush administration policies than counterparts in Europe and the Middle East. Most notably, China's government dropped in mid-2001 its strong emphasis against U.S. "hegemonism" that had prevailed for more than a decade.

Meanwhile, the large powers of Asia, including India, seem to have less of a sense than some West European powers of being key stakeholders in the prevailing international system. They benefit from and participate in the system, but they are more flexible than West European powers in considering alternatives raised by U.S. unilateral actions and other developments. Asian governments also are more interested than ever in multilateral mechanisms to deal with regional,

---

*This chapter was prepared with the participation of Stanley R. Sloan and Casimir A. Yost.

especially economic, problems. However, prevailing security issues like Korean and the Taiwan issues underline continuing competition and wariness among the Asia powers. This situation makes the U.S. security role in the region essential to most Asian governments. The situation offsets to some degree the Asian governments' concern regarding recent U.S. refusal to be bound by multilateral mechanisms in various world arenas.

Crises for U.S. policy in Korea, involving U.S. relations with both North and South Korea, seem unlikely to be resolved soon or satisfactorily. The Taiwan situation also is unstable. The process for dealing with the Korean crises and possible difficulties in Taiwan likely will preoccupy U.S. policy in Asia, and on balance probably will weaken U.S. leadership in the region. Nevertheless, the crises appear likely to remain manageable for U.S. policy, particularly given the continued broad strengths in U.S. power and influence in Asia. Those strengths will continue to support U.S. regional leadership, notably in the war on terrorism, and regional stability and development compatible with American interests.

If protracted Korean crises and tensions in Taiwan were to combine with other significant complications for U.S. policy, it would be more difficult for the U.S. government to manage the crises smoothly, and it would increase the likelihood of disruption of U.S. interests in Asia. Those complications include the failure of U.S. policy toward Iraq, the failure of governance in Pakistan and Afghanistan, a possible major terrorist attack on the United States, a possible India-Pakistan war, and/or a major U.S. economic downturn.

Introduction: Growing U.S. Stake in Asia

U.S. interests in Asia[1] are strong and growing. Strategically and economically, Asia—especially East Asia—has occupied for many years the top rung in U.S. foreign policy concerns, roughly comparable to U.S. interest in Europe. The shift in U.S. strategic orientation as a result of the war on terrorism has resulted in a marked upswing in U.S. interest and involvement in South and Central Asia, and renewed activism in Southeast Asia, reinforcing the long-standing U.S. position as Asia's dominant power.

At least since the disaster of Pearl Harbor, U.S. leaders have recognized that a hostile power dominating East Asia poses a direct threat to the United States. Thus, U.S. policy since that time has sought a favorable balance of power in the region. This has involved strenuous efforts including the bloody, protracted conflicts against Japanese aggression and communist military expansion in Korea and Vietnam; massive expenditure of U.S. military resources and economic assistance in prolonged efforts to balance and contain Soviet, Chinese, and other communist influence; and the continued maintenance of active defense alliances and about one hundred thousand U.S. military forces in the region following the collapse of the Soviet Union and the end of the Cold War.[2]

East Asia, like Europe, is one of the U.S.'s leading trading partners. The Southeast Asian economies were weakened by the Asian economic crisis of 1997–1998, and the Japanese economy—the second largest in the world—has seen little vibrant growth for more than a decade. However, overall Asian growth has remained impressive as the regional economies have recovered from the economic crisis. With growth rates averaging above 8 percent a year, China has loomed particularly prominently as the world's largest recipient of foreign investment and the locus of U.S. and other international manufacturing and processing activities for world markets. East Asia receives about 25 percent of U.S. exports and provides about one-third of U.S. imports, resulting in large U.S. trade deficits with the region.[3]

The rapid economic growth of Asia has provided a basis for ever-increasing cultural and other informal U.S.-Asian interchange. U.S. policy has sought with varying degrees of intensity to reinforce this trend, looking to promote greater democracy, human rights, and other U.S.-backed norms of governance. The collapse of communist regimes in the U.S.S.R. and other countries added to the anti-authoritarian trends in several Asian states. Major political liberalization took place in the 1980s in the Philippines, Korea, Taiwan, and Mongolia. Upsurges of demands for democratic reform also swept China and Burma late in that decade but were suppressed by force. The Asian economic crisis in the late 1990s so challenged the prevailing order in Indonesia that pressures for democracy became unstoppable, resulting in a new but uncertain political transition in Indonesia.[4]

Post-Cold War Relations

The collapse of the U.S.S.R. and the end of the Cold War was a victory for the United States, but these events also posed a major challenge for U.S. foreign policy. In the 1990s, Americans demonstrated deep divisions over foreign policy, and contending policy perspectives could not be bridged to develop a coherent policy toward Asia or other important areas. Because security issues and opposition to Soviet expansion no longer drove U.S. foreign policy, economic interest, democratization abroad, and human rights gained greater prominence. Various pressure groups and other institutions interested in these and other subjects, like environmental and transnational issues, also enhanced influence in policymaking. Historically, such fluidity and competition among priorities have more often than not been the norm in U.S. foreign policy. The requirements of the Cold War were effective in establishing rigor and order in U.S. foreign policy priorities, but that era was over. In particular, the post-Cold War period saw substantial changes in the way foreign policy was made in the United States. In general, there was a shift away from the elitism of the past and toward much greater pluralism. This increased the opportunity for input by nongovernmental or lobby groups with a wide range of interests in foreign policy.[5]

The divisions among Americans over foreign policy during this period were seen in contending schools of thought prominent among U.S. leaders, interest groups, and elite and popular opinion. [6]

One school reflected a sense of relative decline of U.S. power and called for the United States to work harder to preserve important interests while adjusting to limited resources and reduced influence. This school argued that these circumstances required the United States to work closely with traditional allies and associates and to seek the cooperation of other major power centers, notably China. It favored toning down post-Cold War U.S. emphasis on human rights and economic and environmental issues with China and other Asian powers in the interests of establishing a broadly compatible relationship with them.

A second school argued for major cutbacks in U.S. international activity, including military involvement and open trade exchanges seen as disadvantageous to the United States. It called for a renewed focus on solving U.S. domestic problems. It wanted to cut back sharply the one hundred thousand U.S. forces in the region and favored protectionist measures against Asian exports.

A third school of thought became much stronger and more dominant as U.S. economic conditions improved later in the 1990s and government spending resumed increases amid budget surpluses. It argued that policy needed to promote a wide range of U.S. interests in international political, military, and economic affairs more actively and to use U.S. influence to pressure countries that did not conform to the norms of an appropriate world order. Supporters of this position wanted the United States to maintain military forces with worldwide capabilities, to lead strongly in world affairs, and to minimize compromises and accommodations. They pressed for democracy and human rights, opposed economic or trading policies of other countries seen as inequitable or predatory, and pushed against proliferation of weapons of mass destruction. Some argued for sanctions against countries that practice coercive birth control, seriously pollute the environment, or harbor terrorists and promote the drug trade. As a consequence, they believed the United States should be more assertive in promoting humanitarian relief and in recognizing the legitimacy of people's right to self-determination. Chinese policies were a big target for these groups, but the pressure also prompted serious controversy in U.S. policy toward Japan, India, and other Asian governments. After the September 11 terrorist attack on America in 2001, this approach to U.S. foreign policy became even more prominent, as Americans for a time put aside differences in focusing in a sometimes strident and uncompromising way on what appeared to be a protracted struggle against world terrorism.

In Asia, meanwhile, the post-Cold War period witnessed the rise of a variety of transnational forces that seriously challenged nation states. The government in Pakistan remained under tremendous pressure from economic, demographic, political, and other sources. Transnational forces of economic globalization and political pluralism seriously weakened the authoritarian Suharto government in Indonesia and complicated the prospects for its successors. Many other Southeast Asian governments and also Japan and other states in Asia had serious difficulties reviving economies in the face of the strong international competition associated with economic globalization.

Nevertheless, the nation-state continued to be the key actor in Asian regional dynamics. Assertive nationalism characterized most countries. Their populations tended to look to the governments to protect their nation's interests and meet their concerns. In general, the post-Cold War period saw greater assertiveness and nationalism on the part of most Asian governments. One result was a slowness and wariness in movement toward regional cooperation. The governments remained at odds over important nationalistic issues, notably significant territorial issues focused on the disputed South China Sea islands but also involving disputed territory between China and Japan, Japan and South Korea, Russia and Japan, and others. Taiwan was in a class by itself in this regard.

Regional rivalries, notably between China and Japan and China and India, also made regional cooperation on security issues difficult. The governments were less wary of regional cooperation in other areas, notably economics, opening the way by the end of the 1990s to some significant developments under the auspices of ASEAN Plus Three—the ten members of the Association of Southeast Asian nations plus China, Japan, and South Korea, among others.

Other general trends characterizing Asia included an upswing in the overall power and influence of the region relative to its power and influence during the Cold War. Though many economic and political issues persisted, the countries in the region as a whole showed more assertiveness based on economic achievement and strong nationalism. The government leaders also tended to eschew strong ideologies. They endeavored to legitimate their rule with generally pragmatic policies focused on economic development and nation building.

Post-Cold War Challenges and Opportunities for U.S. Interests and Policies

The post-Cold War challenges and opportunities for the United States in Asia were determined in considerable measure by prevailing security, economic, and political trends prompted by five categories of factors influencing regional dynamics. Those categories were the following:

1. *Changing regional power relationships and trends.* Since 1990, this included the rise of China, Japan's stagnation, Indonesia's declining power and influence, and the more active role in regional affairs played by Russia, India, the European Union, and other powers outside the region.

2. *The changing dynamics on the Korean peninsula,* characterized by the off-again, on-again thaw in North-South Korean relations and North Korea's nuclear weapons programs and its varying engagement in international affairs.

3. *Economic concerns.* These focused on the difficulty in sustaining economic growth in the highly competitive global economic environment.

4. *The challenge of freer information flows* to both authoritarian regimes and non-authoritarian governments.

5. *Uncertainty in the region concerning U.S. policy.* At times, regional leaders saw signs of U.S. withdrawal or preoccupation elsewhere. At other times, they saw evidence of U.S. unilateralism and intervention. Both were viewed as disruptive to regional stability.

These five categories of factors influencing regional dynamics led to several important trends that the United States dealt with in seeking effective policies in the region. Several factors created an uncertain security environment. It was not so uncertain that countries felt a need to seek close alignment with a major power or with one another to protect themselves. But it prompted a wide variety of "hedging"—each government sought more diverse and varied arrangements in order to shore up its security interests. All powers wanted generally positive relations with the United States but sought diversified ties to enhance their security options. They continued to differ on a strong U.S. regional security presence, with China notably encouraging a gradual weakening of the U.S. position as it sought expanded regional influence, while most others backed a strong U.S. presence.

Asian governments offered mixed support to the U.S. antiterrorism campaign. The U.S. war against the Taliban and the widespread U.S. involvement and deployment in Central, South, and Southeast Asia appeared justified to many Asian governments and their popular and elite opinion. The assertive U.S. policy against Saddam Hussein in Iraq and the U.S. military-led assault on Iraq prompted much stronger anti-U.S. demonstrations and sharp criticism from many Asian governments. Few of the Asian governments, however, departed from their generally pragmatic nation-building efforts that saw little use in a major dispute with the United States over the war.

This gap between more pragmatic government policy and strident anti-U.S. sentiment by popular and elite opinion was difficult to manage for several Asian governments. China's effective control of the official media and other mechanisms allowed Beijing to pursue a moderate stance against U.S. policies, in stark contrast with China's frequent outbursts against U.S. "hegemonism" during the previous decade. Japanese, Indian, South Korea, Australian, Philippine, Thai, and other leaders alienated important constituencies by adopting more moderate and supportive stances toward the Bush administration than their electorates. The strong anti-U.S. opinion in predominantly Muslim countries clearly affected those governments' willingness to be closely associated with the antiterrorist efforts of the United States. Meanwhile, many Asian states appeared more concerned about the implications of the aggressive U.S. stance in Iraq for an escalating dispute between the United States and North Korea over North Korea's nuclear weapons program and were reassured by the generally consultative and moderate approach taken by the Bush government on this issue in 2003–04.

Meanwhile, the challenge of economic globalization caused regional states over time to band together in order to channel and regulate the consequences of increasingly pervasive free-market economic competition. While generally recognizing the need to conform to international economic norms, Asian governments, especially East Asian governments, sought to block or slow perceived adverse consequences of economic globalization by greater cooperation with similarly affected governments in and outside the region in existing organizations like ASEAN, the Asia-Pacific Economic Cooperation group (APEC), and the World Trade Organization (WTO), and in emerging regional and broader groupings, notably the ASEAN Plus Three. National rivalries and other regional differences were less of an obstacle than in the past to East Asian multilateral economic cooperation. These rivalries and differences remained more of an obstacle to multilateral cooperation over more sensitive security issues, however.

The opportunities for the United States posed by these regional trends and developments focused on the continuing broad regional support for close economic engagement with the United States and for a continued strong U.S. military commitment to the region. But these regional trends and developments also posed challenges for U.S. policy. Heading the list were security dilemmas regarding regional hot spots like Korea and Taiwan. The changing regional power alignments and developments on the Korean Peninsula seriously complicated U.S. alliance relations. Though the Bush administration gave high priority to alliance ties with Japan, South Korea, and others, the fact remained that the publics and elites in these countries—especially South Korea—had deeply ambivalent feelings about aspects of the alliance relation.

U.S. policymakers also faced broad pressure in the United States to pursue vigorous free-market policies and to seek to spread democracy and improved human rights practices abroad. This often did not mesh smoothly with Asian leaders trying to control the disruptive consequences of economic globalization, the free flow of information, and perceived political challenges to stability.

Experienced observers pointed out that the types of challenges facing U.S. policymakers in post-Cold War Asia (e.g., managing alliance relations, dealing with security hot spots, and handling differences over economic policies and human rights) were not new or much worse than in past decades. What had changed from the past was the coherence and salience of U.S. policy after the Cold War. During the Cold War, U.S. leaders tended to pay close attention to developments in key world areas and were prone to guard against allowing U.S. domestic interests to influence U.S. foreign policy in ways contrary to broadly accepted U.S. strategic goals. After the end of the Cold War, the consensus in U.S. foreign policy broke down, and U.S. domestic debate and domestic interests and groups had a much stronger role to play in the making of U.S. foreign policy, including policy toward Asia. As a result, U.S. leaders had to work harder in order to establish a proper balance between U.S. domestic and foreign concerns in the making of U.S. policy toward the region.

The terrorist attack on America on September 11, 2001, sharply reduced the salience of post-Cold War U.S. domestic debate over foreign policy. The U.S. campaign against the Taliban and broader U.S. military and other involvement in various parts of Asia enjoyed broad bipartisan support. U.S. domestic criticism of the Bush administration's firmer line on China dissipated, as the policy resulted in a marked improvement in U.S.-China ties. U.S. domestic criticism of the administration's hard line on North Korea also declined for a while, though it began to reemerge as the U.S. administration followed its initial success in military operations in Afghanistan with strong rhetoric and military preparations specifically targeted against Saddam Hussein in Iraq and also including North Korea and Iran. The Bush administration's decision to initiate a military attack in Iraq without the support of key allies or the full support of the United Nations saw some strong U.S. domestic opposition, which grew as the United States became bogged down in a protracted and expensive effort to stabilize post-war Iraq amid continued international rebukes of perceived U.S. unilateralism and attempts at domination.

Recent Controversies

The overall Bush administration's record in Asia and the outlook for U.S. policy over the next few years are matters of debate among specialists.[7] Many particularly criticize the Bush government for mishandling Korean issues; for issuing unilateralist policy declarations adding to tension in the region; and for a lack of attention to economic, environmental, and multilateral measures seen as important to long-range Asian stability and smooth U.S.-Asian relations. They sometimes predict dire consequences, most immediately involving dangerous nuclear proliferation, war on the Korean Peninsula, rupture of U.S. alliance relations with South Korea, and confrontation with China and others. Some add that the Bush administration's tendency to "preempt" threats by attacking first could set a bad precedent for such Asian hotspots as the Taiwan Strait and Kashmir.

North Korea took provocative actions in late 2002 and 2003, breaking declared non-proliferation commitments and reactivating nuclear facilities frozen under the 1994 U.S.-North Korea Agreed Framework accord. This posed a major challenge for U.S. policy that was not well anticipated by the U.S. government. Bush administration reaction was complicated by deep division within the administration over how to handle North Korea and by strong differences in U.S.-South Korean policy toward North Korea and broader alliance relations.[8] Tensions in U.S.-South Korean alliance relations and anti-American sentiment in South Korea rose markedly during the Bush administration and were important factors in the election of South Korea's new president in December 2002. Subsequent U.S. and South Korean efforts to ease tensions, bridge differences, and solidify relations remained awkward in 2003–04 and added to the arguments of those claiming that the U.S.-South Korean alliance was in crisis and poised for a major change in the next few years.[9]

Significant additional problems for U.S. policy in Asia came as Asian elite and public opinion joined the worldwide complaints against U.S. unilateral actions and dominance in international affairs seen at the time of the U.S.-led attack on Iraq and repeated U.S. policy declarations supporting preemptive actions against adversaries.[10] The *Far Eastern Economic Review* cited a June 2003 study by the Pew Research Center for the People and the Press to assert that "the image of the United States plummeted in the wake of the war in Iraq." Only 15 percent of Indonesians polled in spring 2003 had a positive view of the United States, down from 75 percent in 2000. Most Indonesians polled attributed their negative views about the United States to the policies and behavior of President Bush. A major decline also took place among South Koreans and Pakistanis. In all three countries, support for the U.S.-led war on terrorism was under 30 percent.[11] A January 2004 poll showed that more South Koreans saw the United States as a greater threat to Korean security than North Korea.[12]

Chinese popular opinion had been against the U.S. action in Iraq, and later polls showed that Chinese opinion favored a UN refusal to support the post-war U.S. reconstruction efforts in Iraq, arguing that "when the United States decided to invade Iraq, it held the UN in contempt" and a UN rebuff would teach the United States "a profound lesson." The vast majority of Chinese urban dwellers polled in September 2003 said they admired France and Germany for standing up to the United States over the Iraq war.[13]

In Southeast Asia, government leaders took account of the strongly negative view of the U.S. attack on Iraq on the part of Muslim populations, notably in Indonesia and Malaysia. The Indonesian foreign minister delivered a strong rebuke of U.S. policy in Iraq at an international meeting in Jakarta in December 2003.[14] Indonesian President Megawati Sukarnoputri allowed police and security forces to cooperate with U.S., Australian, and other officials to solve the 2002 Bali bombing case, but she maintained some distance from the overall U.S. war on terrorism. Megawati faces an election in May 2004 and needs support from Muslim parties. In Malaysia, Prime Minister Mahatir sharply criticized the United States for inflaming radical movements without addressing root causes of terrorism.[15]

Antipathy to the U.S. assault on Iraq and perceived disregard for UN prerogatives elicited large-scale demonstrations and other actions in Australia, South Korea, Japan, India, and elsewhere, indicating that even U.S. allies and Asian government leaders leaning to support President Bush had to take account of strong elite and popular opinion moving in anti-American directions. It was widely held that the U.S. leadership and President Bush in particular were not well aware of the decline of previously favorable attitudes in Asia toward the United States and the strong, hostile reactions to the U.S. attack on Iraq.[16]

In late 2003, Taiwan emerged as a trouble spot for U.S. policy during the lead up to Taiwan's presidential election. The Taiwan presidential election campaign of 2003–2004 saw incumbent President Chen Shui-bian win reelection in March 2004 with a campaign emphasizing Taiwan's determination to confront China's military buildup and other pressure tactics and to develop a legal status independent of China. In subsequent statements to the media and to his supporters preparing for hotly contested legislative elections in December 2004, Chen repeatedly affirmed his determination to pursue greater independence. Beijing had hoped the more moderate opposition candidates would have won the presidential election and viewed Chen's plans with alarm, warning of China's determination to resort to force if necessary.[17]

In this situation of renewed tension and potential crisis in China-Taiwan relations, the Bush administration showed no slackening in its efforts to provide military support for Taiwan, to deploy forces to Guam, and to make other arrangements needed to deter China from using force against Taiwan. At the same time, U.S. officials gave much more emphasis to the administration's resolve to press the Chen Shui-bian administration against taking legal or other steps that could provoke a military confrontation in Taiwan. President Bush met the visiting Chinese premier on December 9, 2003, and used the occasion to go on record against efforts by the Taiwan government to take unilateral steps to alter the status quo in Taiwan-China relations.

Controversies in Perspective—U.S. Strengths in Asia

While the impact of the recent controversies and criticisms of U.S. policies toward Iraq, the United Nations, Korea, and other issues remain important, they probably should be balanced by appropriate attention to the many continuing favorable trends in Asia for U.S. policy and interests. The result leads to an overall generally positive assessment of continued U.S. leadership in promoting stability, development, and U.S. values in the region.

As detailed below, this result depends on the absence of a major U.S. policy failure in Southwest Asia, Korea, Taiwan, and U.S. homeland defense, among others, or a serious U.S. economic decline. U.S. policy failure or economic collapse would lead to a perception of U.S. weakness that could prompt adversaries and others to confront and challenge U.S. interests in Asia and elsewhere.

At a time of U.S. preoccupation with Iraq and other priorities, the Bush administration has adjusted in generally pragmatic ways to unexpected Asian challenges, notably in the Korean Peninsula—an area of much more salient concern than Iraq to most Asian governments. While repeatedly justifying the principle of U.S. preemption and unilateral action in other parts of the world, the Bush administration in practice has sought to deal with the North Korean crisis and other issues in Asia through broad international consultation and engagement. Of course, North Korea's ongoing efforts to develop nuclear weapons continue and could precipitate sharp divisions between the United States and Asian powers or within the U.S. government.

Several key strengths prevail in U.S.-Asian relations that support the U.S. administration's ability to manage Asian crises and to sustain U.S. leadership in promoting stability, development, and U.S. values in Asia.[18] Government leaders on both sides of the Pacific continue to put a high value on the U.S. security commitment and military presence in Asia. U.S. resolve to remain actively involved in regional security has been strengthened by U.S. government efforts after the September 11, 2001 terrorist attack on America. The strong U.S. military presence is generally welcomed by Asian government leaders, and even Chinese leaders have notably modified their past criticism of the U.S. security role.[19]

Debate over the size and deployment of U.S. forces in South Korea has become a key element in the crises facing U.S. policy on the Korean Peninsula. Nevertheless, the South Korean and U.S. governments appear determined to manage the debate without jeopardizing strong mutual interests supported by a continued U.S. military presence in South Korea.[20] U.S. officials took pains to reassure South Korea and others in Asia that the proposed realignment of U.S. forces on the Korean Peninsula, and the broader U.S. realignment of forces abroad, would enhance, not reduce, U.S. ability to deter and defeat foes. These assurances had more weight, as they came after the impressive U.S. military victories in Afghanistan and Iraq.[21] Meanwhile, the 2003 polls that showed setbacks for the U.S. image in certain countries in Asia also showed that most of those polled retained overall positive views of U.S. leadership and that clear majorities in Asia agreed that their interests would suffer if the United States were no longer the world's dominant power.[22]

The Bush administration has a less activist international economic policy than the Clinton administration, but the United States maintains open markets despite aberrations such as moves in 2002 to protect U.S. farmers and steel manufacturers. U.S. open-market policy is welcomed by Asian governments that view the U.S. economy as more important to Asian economic well-being, especially after the Asian economic crisis and Japan's persisting stagnation. Though China is a new engine of regional growth, U.S. economic prospects remain much more important for Asian development. The United States in recent years has absorbed an increasing percentage (about 40 percent, according to U.S. government figures) of the exports from China, which is emerging as the export-manufacturing base for investors from a wide range of advanced Asian economies. The U.S. market continues to absorb one third of the exports of Japan. The economies of South Korea, Taiwan, and ASEAN rely on the U.S. market to receive around 20 percent of their exports. Meanwhile, U.S. direct foreign investment has grown notably in China; the level there is less than U.S. investment in Australia, Hong Kong, Singapore, or Japan, however.[23]

After the Cold War, strong U.S. domestic pressure pushed democracy, human rights, and other U.S. values in Asia and met resistance from authoritarian governments seeking to preserve their ruling prerogatives and Asian democracies fearing regional instability. Despite strong rhetorical emphasis, Bush administration policy has been pragmatic, especially as the United States sought allies and supporters in the global war on terrorism and other endeavors. This adjustment generally is welcomed in Asia and has worked to ease U.S. differences with authoritarian governments in Asia.[24]

The United States held the preeminent power position in the region, especially after September 11, 2001. U.S. power appeared to belie predictions in earlier decades of an inevitable U.S. decline, as the United States became more powerful and influential in Asia and the Pacific than at any time since the defeat of Japan in World War II. In the face of protracted violence and mounting U.S. casualties in Iraq in 2003–04, there has been growing concern over possible U.S. "overreach"—stretching military and economic commitments beyond U.S. capabilities. Amid criticism by some U.S. nongovernment experts and grumblings in the ranks of the U.S. military, U.S. defense planners moved ahead with planned realignment and downsizing of U.S. forces in Asia and elsewhere abroad, while sustaining large ground force commitments in Iraq. The realignment reportedly involved plans to downsize U.S. forces in Western Europe and Korea, to increase the mobility of U.S. forces abroad, and to expand the scope of U.S. bases and access points abroad while reducing the overall size of U.S. bases abroad.[25] On balance, the changes did not appear to change the prevailing situation where some in the Asian region might wish to challenge or confront the United States and might be more inclined to do so if the United States were seen as "bogged down" in Iraq; but most remained reluctant to do so, given the dangers they would face in opposing the world's dominant power, with a leadership seemingly prepared to use that power against its enemies.[26]

The asymmetry of power between the U.S. and Asian governments probably will not change soon. U.S.-realigned military forces in Asia, backed by the unsurpassed U.S. military capabilities demonstrated in recent conflicts in Europe and Asia, seem well positioned to deal with regional contingencies. The massive size and overall importance of the U.S. economy to Asian economic well-being has risen in the post-Cold War period in the eyes of Asian governments seeking international outreach and economic development as a foundation for their conventional nation-building strategies. U.S. protectionist measures in response to large trade deficits and U.S. job losses probably would dampen Asian enthusiasm for closer ties to the U.S. market and reduce U.S. influence in the region, however.

The major regional powers, including stagnating Japan and such rising powers as China and India, are domestically preoccupied and are likely to remain so for some time to come.[27] Focused on internal issues, they seek support from the United States and other powers and do not want difficulties in their foreign relations. In theory, however, there is a danger that the Asian powers may align against the United States and its interests in significant ways. The Asian nations, including leading regional powers Japan, China, and India, are actively maneuvering and hedging, seeking new and more multifaceted arrangements to secure their interests in the uncertain regional environment. They sometimes cooperate together in broader arrangements like Sino-Japanese cooperation in ASEAN Plus Three. ASEAN Plus Three promotes U.S.-backed goals of regional cooperation, though some Americans are wary of such regional arrangements that exclude the United States. At bottom, however, the Asian nations—especially the leading powers—are divided by deep suspicions, indicating that any meaningful cooperation seriously detrimental to U.S. interests remains unlikely.[28]

U.S. policymakers also have done a better job in managing the often-strong U.S. domestic pressures that in the post-Cold War period tended to drive U.S. policy in extreme directions detrimental to a sound and balanced approach to Asia. President Clinton's engagement policy toward China in his second term was more coherent than the policy in his first term that appeared driven by competing U.S. domestic interests. Moreover, President Bush's policy is better suited to mainstream U.S. opinion regarding China and has the added advantage of avoiding the need for significant U.S. concessions toward China on sensitive issues like Taiwan that seriously exacerbate the U.S. domestic debate about China policy.[29] And President Bush's attention to Japan has reduced Japanese concerns caused by the Clinton administration's emphasis on China and its tough public criticism of Japan's economic policies, avoiding U.S. domestic controversy over this policy area.[30]

A major U.S. weakness—more important in Asia than the Bush administration's aggressive policy regarding Iraq and other world issues—remains the Bush administration's tough stance toward North Korea, which poses obvious and serious difficulties for U.S. influence in Asia. The difficulty of meshing a tough U.S. stance toward North Korea while supporting South Korea's asymmetrical engagement efforts with Pyongyang has not been fully addressed. For a time, U.S. policy drifted, with leaders in Washington and much of the rest of the world focused on other, more immediate problems. North Korean brinksmanship in 2002–03, however, brought the issue to a head, forcing the United States to act. There remains a possibility for unilateral, forceful U.S. actions, including a military attack on North Korea. The danger that Bush administration hard-liners, however, would push policy to an extreme and create a major crisis in U.S.-Asia relations is mitigated to some degree by strong countervailing opinion in the administration and more broadly in the Congress, the media, and among U.S. experts and opinion leaders warning of the dire consequences of excessive U.S. pressure on the North Korean regime.[31]

The United States and the Asian Powers

The Bush administration's success in improving U.S. relations with all the great powers in Asia adds to the strength of U.S. leadership in the region, and reinforces the U.S. government's ability to deal with crises on the Korean Peninsula and other regional difficulties. The likelihood of United States having good relations with Japan and China at the same time is very rare. The United States being the dominant power in South Asia and having good relations with both India and Pakistan is unprecedented, as is the current U.S. maintenance of good relations with both Beijing and Taipei.

The administration came to power with plans to markedly enhance the political-military partnership with Japan. The Japanese government of Prime Minister Junichiro Koizumi was a responsive partner, though constraints posed by Japanese economic stagnation and political differences in Japan have limited cooperation to some degree. Japan provided strong support in the war on terrorism, including an unprecedented Indian Ocean naval deployment in support of allied operations in the war in Afghanistan. Prime Minister Koizumi was outspoken in backing the U.S.-led attack on Saddam Hussein and deployed hundreds of Japanese forces to Iraq. Koizumi may have diverged from U.S. interests in meeting Kim Jong Il in September 2002, but he found common ground with the Bush administration in its subsequent efforts to deal with North Korea's provocative nuclear weapons development. [32]

Compared with traditional U.S. allies, India's government was less critical and more understanding of Bush administration policy regarding sensitive issues in missile defense, arms control, the United Nations, and the war in Iraq. It welcomed the U.S. administration's plans for a greater Indian role in Asian security and world affairs, and the steadily expanding U.S. military relationship with India. The terrorist attacks of September 11, 2001, proved to be a catalyst in improving U.S.-Indian relations.[33] The Indian parliament supported strong popular and elite opposition to U.S. intervention in Iraq, but the Indian administration was more circumspect.

The improvement of U.S. relations with Russia seen in the first Bush-Putin summit in the months before the terrorist attack on America was markedly enhanced by U.S.-Russian cooperation after September 11, 2001. Russia saw its interests served by fostering closer economic and strategic cooperation with the United States and the West and by playing down past major differences over U.S. missile defense programs and NATO enlargement. Maneuvering in the United Nations in the months prior to the war in Iraq saw Russia join with France and others in standing against U.S. military actions to topple Saddam Hussein without renewed UN approval. After the U.S.-led coalition succeeded militarily in Iraq and senior Bush administration officials made significant gestures to ease tensions with Moscow, Russia appeared prepared to resume a more cooperative stance toward the United States.[34]

The breakthrough in U.S. relations with China was by far the most important success for Bush administration policy in Asia. The rapid rise of China's power and influence in world affairs, especially around China's periphery in Asia, initially received negative Bush administration attention and prompted a steady stream of U.S. media, congressional, and other commentary warning of People's Republic of China (PRC) efforts to push the United States out of Asia. In contrast, actual Chinese behavior in the region and in improving relations with the Bush administration seemed to underscore strong awareness by Chinese leaders of the difficulties involved in China's competing directly with the U.S. superpower.[35]

The power and the policies of the George W. Bush administration indeed did change the Asian situation in important and sometimes negative respects for Chinese interests, especially after the September 11, 2001, terrorist attack on America. Chinese leaders nonetheless reacted with restraint and moderation—helping to set the stage for a significant upswing in U.S.-China relations over Asian and other issues. U.S. specialists held different views about what factors were most important in causing the favorable turn in U.S.-China relations since mid-2001, but they tended to agree that the improvement in U.S.-Chinese relations reinforced Beijing's moderate trend in policy toward the United States, Asia, and world affairs.[36]

Outlook

The large-scale deployment of U.S. military forces and other government resources to the U.S.-led occupation in Iraq along with the concurrent U.S. pressures against Iran and initiatives elsewhere in the Middle East seem to ensure that U.S. government strategic emphasis will focus on southwest Asia for many years. Stabilizing Iraq and avoiding negative trends in the Persian Gulf and the Middle East following the toppling of Saddam Hussein represent large tasks for U.S. leaders. Building and maintaining international coalitions to help with peacekeeping, reconstruction, and establishing good government in Iraq require U.S. officials to engage in attentive diplomacy and other persuasive efforts in the face of widespread international antipathy to the U.S. decision to launch the war against Iraq without the full endorsement of the UN Security Council.

The Bush administration's strong stance against Iran focused on charges regarding Teheran's support for terrorism and nuclear weapons development. During and after the war to topple Saddam Hussein, Bush administration officials took repeated aim at Iran, as well as Syria, for actions contrary to U.S. interests. Nevertheless, the protracted and violent struggle between the Israeli government and Palestinian opponents complicated U.S. policy in the region; U.S. strong support for Israel added to difficulties for U.S. policy among Islamic states and peoples. Meanwhile, the administration's strong push for greater democracy in the Middle East received mixed reactions, especially from conservative U.S. allies and associates in the Middle East.[37]

Popular and elite opinion in much of the world opposed the U.S. war and demonstrated broader concerns about U.S. dominance and "hegemony" in world affairs. France, Germany, Russia, and governments in the Middle East and much of the Muslim world strongly criticized the U.S. decision to attack Iraq. In much of Asia, however, the governments stood at odds with their publics and nongovernment elites and reacted more pragmatically in dealing with the United States over the Iraq war and broader concerns flowing from U.S. international dominance. Prime Minister Koizumi was outspoken in support of Japan's U.S. ally, quick to lend military support within the confines of Japan's existing constraints on deployments abroad, and prominent in leading the postwar aid effort. South Korea's new president pushed a reluctant parliament to approve the deployment of several thousand troops to Iraq, repeatedly stressing the importance for South Korea of preserving a close alliance relationship with the United States in the face of North Korea's provocations. Chinese leaders showed little interest in being associated closely with international resistance to U.S. leadership in Iraq, however. Similarly, India's government remained restrained in criticizing the U.S. attack on Iraq.[38]

Contingencies could seriously weaken U.S. policy in Asia. They include possible setbacks in the war on terrorism involving large-scale terrorist attacks, possibly including weapons of mass destruction, against U.S. or allied targets, and regime failure in such frontline states as Afghanistan or Pakistan, where political conditions and governance remain unstable and weak. A major—possibly nuclear—war between India and Pakistan, precipitated by disputes over Kashmir or other issues, would be disastrous for regional peace and stability. World economic trends remain uncertain, with the U.S. economy among those grappling with recovery and large-scale government budget and trade deficits. If past practice is any guide, major setbacks in the pace and scope of the U.S. economic recovery are likely to prompt heavy partisan attack, as U.S. leaders seeking to unseat President Bush in the 2004 election target the costs to the United States of the Bush administration's wide ranging military deployments abroad.[39]

The crisis with North Korea presents a continuing, serious problem for U.S. policy in Asia.[40] Recent U.S. policy regarding North Korea buys time and keeps South Korea and other powers in an ostensibly common front, but it does not resolve North Korea's nuclear weapons development or deep U.S. differences with South Korea, China, and others at home and abroad on how to deal with North Korea. Under a second Bush administration, negotiations and other aspects of U.S. and international efforts to deal with North Korea may have episodes of improvement in U.S. relations with concerned powers and episodes of crisis brought on by North Korea's brinksmanship or other factors. The process is likely to be prolonged because of the mix of North Korean rigidity and frequent brinksmanship, Bush refusal to be blackmailed, and seemingly insufficient U.S. power/influence to coerce the North. U.S. alliance management (notably, relations with South Korea) and great power diplomacy (notably, relations with China) over this issue will be complicated and probably difficult. The Bush administration's ability to manage U.S. domestic critics may also be challenged, especially at times of tension with North Korea. Overall, the process promises to preoccupy and weaken U.S. leadership in Asian affairs.

A more assertive U.S. policy, presumably involving U.S. pressure or perhaps military attack, remains possible, though such an assertive U.S. stance faces North Korea's military power and the strong opposition of key powers—especially South Korea and China. Also possible but not likely is the Bush administration's offering major concessions to the North, without a clear path to the North's denuclearization, in order to ease the crisis and meet demands of South Korea, China, and U.S. domestic critics.

Regarding the Taiwan straits, Chinese leaders seem constrained by U.S. power. They also have not given up hope that Chinese economic blandishments, diplomatic pressures, and military intimidation, and newly apparent U.S. pressures on Taiwan, will constrain Taiwan's leaders from de jure independence.[41] For their part, Taiwan leaders seek initiatives in cross strait or international relations, sometimes even at the risk of disrupting the prevailing modus vivendi in cross strait ties. The Bush administration in the recent past has come down hard against Taiwan leaders who risk such disruption, and the fear of alienating U.S. support may be sufficient to curb possible Taiwan actions that might provoke a harsh response from China.[42]

Southeast Asia is an area of serious concern in the war on terrorism but appears to hold few major problems for U.S. policy, though managing sometimes difficult U.S. security ties with countries like Indonesia and the Philippines represents a complication in the broader U.S. war on terrorism. As noted earlier, there remains the distinct possibility of such major failures for U.S. policy in Asia as a government collapse in Afghanistan or Pakistan, or a war between India and Pakistan; there appears to be too much at stake for U.S. leaders not to give a high priority to diplomatic and other efforts to prevent such negative outcomes in Central and South Asia.

In sum, U.S. assertiveness over Iraq and other issues continues to be widely criticized among Asian popular and elite opinion and has damaged the image of the U.S. government in Asia. Asian governments are reacting pragmatically, however, they remain focused on domestic concerns involving conventional nation building. From their perspective, the crisis posed by North Korea's nuclear weapons development is more important, and the Bush administration thus far is dealing with that issue in a consultative manner acceptable to concerned Asian powers.

Recent U.S. crises in Korea, involving U.S. relations with both North and South Korea, seem unlikely to be resolved soon or satisfactorily. The situation in China-Taiwan relations also could flare into a crisis. The process for dealing with the Korean crises and the Taiwan situation likely will preoccupy U.S. policy in Asia and on balance probably will weaken U.S. leadership in the region. Nevertheless, the crises appear likely to remain manageable for U.S. policy, particularly given the continued broad strengths in U.S. power and influence in Asia. Those strengths will continue to support U.S. regional leadership, notably in the war on terrorism, and regional stability and development compatible with U.S. interests.

Perhaps the greatest longer-term challenge for U.S. officials will involve determining a coherent U.S. policy toward the region. The Bush administration entered office with a relatively clear international security approach to the region, but the war on terrorism, the deep involvement in Iraq, and other circumstances diverted U.S. attention away from significant parts of Asia, resulting in more passive and reactive U.S. positions toward some regional questions (e.g., Korean issues). The role of China in Bush administration strategy has changed markedly, with U.S. policy on North Korea gravitating toward China and with U.S. leaders taking strong positions on Taiwan that are in line with Chinese interests in preserving the status quo in cross strait relations. U.S. involvement in major economic issues in the region has been secondary, with few high-level officials apart from the Special Trade Representative demonstrating substantial regional leadership. U.S. promotion of values like human rights and democracy is mixed, with the administration carefully avoiding actions that would seriously alienate authoritarian Asian leaders important in the U.S. war on terrorism. Meanwhile, policy differences within the administration remain obvious and strong, especially on North Korean issues.

An election victory by Democratic candidate John Kerry would lead to a U.S. administration that also would encounter difficulties in coming up with a coherent regional strategy. One advantage it would have over the Bush administration is that the Democratic president would be in a better position to set policy on the basis of his experience and perspective on the region. Nevertheless, a President Kerry would face the same competing pressures at home and abroad. His ability to deal with them also would be compromised until he is able to field a well-integrated and cooperative foreign policy team. Such a sorting-out process is often marked by confusion, strong personal ambitions, political deal making, and other steps that get in the way of creating coherent foreign policy.

Whatever the orientation of U.S. leaders, they probably will need to mesh their approaches with changing circumstances in the region and in the United States in formulating a well-integrated U.S. policy. In this process, several important questions reflecting the dynamism of Asia and U.S. relations with the region will need to be addressed:

◆ To what degree has recent U.S. preoccupation with the war on terrorism and weapons proliferation modified long-standing U.S. security concerns in Asia and altered U.S. views of an appropriate U.S. military presence and basing structure in Asia?

◆ What is the appropriate balance of preemption and deterrence in U.S. national security policy, and how have changes in U.S. policy giving more emphasis to preemption after September 11, 2001, affected U.S. relations with Asian governments and peoples?

◆ Should U.S. alliance relations remain the centerpiece of U.S. security policy in Asia, or should they be diminished in favor of greater U.S. accommodation of rising powers like China and India and more active reliance on multilateral forums like the ASEAN Regional Forum or the Six Party Talks on North Korea?

◆ Is U.S. preoccupation with combating terrorism leading to a serious decline in U.S. leadership in international economic forums and institutions that are the centerpiece of rising interest in multilateralism in Asia?

◆ Does the strong U.S. emphasis on democracy as an antidote to terrorism complement or complicate U.S. influence and leadership in Asian affairs?

Notes

1. "Asia" in this article includes South and Central Asia but not countries west of Afghanistan and Pakistan.

2. Michael Yahuda, *The International Politics of the Asia-Pacific 1945–1995* (London: Routledge, 1996), 109–157.

3. For analysis on economic trends in East Asia and East Asian relations with the United States and other key world areas see among others *East Asia: Recovery and Beyond* (Washington, D.C.: The World Bank, 2000). See also *East Asia: The Road to Recovery* (Washington, D.C., The World Bank, 1998), and *Economist Intelligence Unit Country Profile* (Annual Report) (London, Economic Intelligence Unit, 2002).

4. Robert Sutter, *The United States and East Asia* (Lanham, MD: Rowman and Littlefield, 2003), 25.

5. Harry Harding, *Public Engagement in American Foreign Policy* (New York: American Assembly, Columbia University, February 1995).

6. For greater detail on these views and other aspects discussed in the rest of this section, see Sutter, *The United States and East Asia*, chapters 1 and 10.

7. Most of the thirteen contributors in an authoritative Woodrow Wilson International Center assessment of the Bush administration's policy toward Asia were sharply critical. See eds. Robert Hathaway and Wilson Lee, *George W. Bush and Asia* (Washington D.C.: Woodrow Wilson International Center for Scholars, 2003). For a more favorable assessment of U.S. policy in Asia, see Satu A. Limaye, "Almost quiet on the Asia-Pacific front," in *Asia-Pacific Responses to U.S. Security Policies* (Honolulu: Asia Pacific Center for Security Studies, 2003), available at http://www.apcss.org/Publications/SAS/SASAPResponse030320/SAS030320APResponse.html. See also *U.S. Strategy in the Asia-Pacific Region* (Washington D.C.: Woodrow Wilson International Center for Scholars, 2003).

8. Nicholas Eberstadt and Joseph Ferguson, "North Korea: The Korean nuclear Crisis" in eds. Richard Ellings, et al., *Strategic Asia 2003–2004* (Seattle: National Bureau of Asian Research, 2003), 131–64.

9. Ralph Cossa, "Diplomacy fails with Iraq; is North Korea next?" and Donald Gross, "Tensions escalate in Korea as the U.S. targets Iraq," in *Comparative Connections* (April 2003), http://www.csis.org/pacfor. Larry Niksch, *Korea: Korea-U.S. relations: issues for Congress*, Issue Brief 98045 (Washington: the Library of Congress, Congressional Research Service, May 5, 2003).

10. What the world thinks in 2002 (Washington, D.C.: The Pew Research Center for the People and the Press, December 2002), http://people-press.org/reports/display.php3?ReportID=165. Raymond Copson (coordinator) *Iraq war: background and issues overview*, Report RL31715 (updated April 22, 2003) (Washington, D.C.: the Library of Congress Congressional Research Service).

11. "Americans out of favour in Asia," *Far Eastern Economic Review* (July 24, 2003), http://www/feer.com (accessed July 24, 2003).

12. *Digital Chosun Ilbo*, January 12, 2004, http://english.chosun.com (accessed January 18, 2004).

13. David Hsieh, "Chinese feel UN should teach U.S. a lesson," *Straits Times* (Singapore), September 17, 2003, http://www.taiwansecurity.org (last accessed September 19, 2003).

14. Raymond Bonner, "Indonesia official rebukes U.S. over Iraq war," *New York Times*, December 8, 2003, http://www.nytimes.com (accessed December 12, 2003).

15. Jay Solomon, "Asian Muslim nations join China to denounce U.S. attack on Iraq," *The Wall Street Journal/WSJ online*, March 20, 2003 (accessed March 21, 2003).

16. David Sanger, "On his high-speed trip, Bush glimpses a perception gap," *New York Times*, October 24, 2003, A1.

17. See articles by Bonnie Glaser and David Brown in *Comparative Connections* (April 2004), http://www.csis.org/pacfor.

18. These are reviewed in more detail in Robert Sutter, "United States: U.S. leadership—prevailing strengths amid challenges," *Strategic Asia*, 36–41. *What the world thinks in 2002*, T–45, T–50.

19. Michael Swaine, "Reverse Course? The Fragile Turnaround in U.S.-China Relations," Policy Brief 22 (Washington, D.C.: Carnegie Endowment for International Peace, February 2003), 1–3. Bonnie Glaser, "China and U.S. disagree, but with smiles," *Comparative Connections* (April 2003). Robert Sutter, "Grading Bush's China Policy," *PACNET* 10 (March 8, 2002), http://www.csis.org/pacfor.

20. Ralph Cossa, "Bush-Roh: Closing the gap," *PACNET* 20 (May 20, 2003), http://www.csis.org/pacfor.

21. Greg Jaffe, "Pentagon Prepares to Scatter Soldiers to Remote Corners," *The Wall Street Journal*, May 27, 2003, 1. Paul Wolfowitz, "Sustaining the U.S. commitment in Asia," *PACNET* 22A (June 5, 2003); and Ralph Cossa, "Force restructuring anxiety," PACNET 22 (June 3, 2003), both available at http://www.csis.org/pacfor.

22. *What the world thinks in 2002*, T–45, T–50.

23. Figures from U.S. Department of Commerce, 2002, 2003. Chinese government figures show Chinese exports to the United States as much less than seen in U.S. government figures.

24. The United States did not seek to bring China's human rights conditions before the UN Human Rights Commission in 2003. George Gedda, "U.S. won't propose resolution on China," *Associated Press*, April 11, 2003 (Internet version).

25. Greg Jaffe, "Pentagon prepares to scatter troops." See also discussion in *U.S. Strategy in the Asia-Pacific Region*.

26. "The acceptability of American power," *Economist*, June 29, 2002 (Internet version). See also G. John Ikenberry, *Strategic Reactions to American Preeminence*, U.S. National Intelligence Council Conference Report (July 28, 2003), available at http://www.odci.gov/nic/confreports_stratreact.html.

27. See the chapters on China, Japan, India, and Russia in *Strategic Asia 2003–2004.*

28. Benjamin Self, "China and Japan: a façade of friendship," *Washington Quarterly* 26:1, (winter 2002–2003): 77–88. Robert Sutter, *The United States and East Asia*, 199–200, 222–23.

29. Hugo Restall, "Tough love for China," *The Wall Street Journal*, October 21, 2002 (Internet version).

30. Richard Cronin (coordinator), *Japan-U.S. Relations: Issue for Congress*, Issue Brief 97004 (updated April 25, 2003) (Washington, D.C.: The Library of Congress, Congressional Research Service).

31. Cossa, "Diplomacy fails with Iraq."

32. Brad Glosserman, "U.S.-Japan relations: how high is up?" *Comparative Connections* (April 2003). John Miller, "The glacier moves: Japan's response to U.S. security policies," in *Asia-Pacific Responses to U.S. security policies* (Honolulu: Asia Pacific Center for Security Studies, 2003) (Internet version).

33. Mohan Malik, "High hopes: India's response to U.S. security policies," in *Asia-Pacific Responses to U.S. security policies* (Honolulu: Asia Pacific Center for Security Studies, 2003) (Internet version).

34. Joseph Ferguson, "U.S.-Russian partnership: a casualty of war?" *Comparative Connections* (April 2003). Rajan Menon, "Why Russia says 'nyet' to the U.S.," *Chicago Tribune* (March 12, 2003) (Internet version). William Wohlforth, "Russia" in eds. Richard Ellings and Aaron Friedberg *Asian Aftershocks: Strategic Asia 2002–2003* (Seattle: NBR 2002), 183–222. William Wohlforth, "Russia: Russia's soft balancing act," in eds. Richard Ellings et al., *Strategic Asia 2003–2004* (Seattle: NBR 2003), 165–180.

35. Andrew Nathan and Bruce Gilley, *China's New Rulers: The Secret Files* (New York: New York Review of Books, 2002), 207–209. Thomas Christensen, "China," in *Asian Aftershocks*, 51–94. Thomas Christensen and Michael Glonsny, "China: Sources of stability in U.S.-China security relations," *Strategic Asia 2003–2004*, 53–80.

36. Swaine, "Reverse Course?" Michael Yahuda, "China's Win-Win Globalization," *YaleGlobal online*, http://www.yaleglobal.yale.edu (accessed February 19, 2003).

37. See the extensive coverage of these issues focused on President Bush's April 13, 2004, press conference in *New York Times*, April 14, 2004, 1. Thomas Donnelly, "Lessons of a three week war," *Weekly Standard*, April 22, 2003. Thomas Donnelly, "Brave New World: an enduring Pax Americana," *AEI (American Enterprise Institute) National Security Outlook* (Washington, D.C.: AEI, April 2003), http://www.aei.org. Condoleezza Rice, "Transforming the Middle East," *Washington Post*, August 7, 2003. George Packer, "Dreaming of Democracy," *New York Times Magazine*, March 2, 2003, 44–49, 60, 90, 104.

38. *Asia-Pacific Responses to U.S. security policies* (Honolulu: Asia Pacific Center for Security Studies, 2003). See articles reviewing U.S. relations with Asian governments in *Comparative Connections*, http://www.csis.org/ pacfor April, July, October 2003, and January 2004.

39. For a review of post-Iraq war issues for the United States, see Copson, *Iraq war: background and issues.*

40. The Bush administration had some success in the immediate aftermath of the war in Iraq in limiting the damage from the crises in U.S. relations with North Korea and in U.S. alliance relations with South Korea, but few predict a quick solution to either set of problems. The crises place U.S. policy on the Korean Peninsula in a reactive stance, responding to sometimes unanticipated events and endeavoring to formulate options that limit the damage to U.S. interests and hold out the possibility of resolution in accord with U.S. interests.

41. U.S. Department of Defense, *Annual Report on the Military Power of the People's Republic of China,* 2002 http://www.defenselink.mil/news/ Jul2002/p07122002_p133-02.html.

42. David Brown, "Chen adopts a more cautious approach," *Comparative Connections* (April 2003). David Brown, "Strains over cross strait relations," *Comparative Connections* (January 2004).

APPENDIX
Potential Surprises from the Use of U.S. Power Post-9/11

In the spring of 2004, the Schlesinger Working Group on Strategic Surprises, part of the Institute for the Study of Diplomacy, convened to discuss the draft papers that compose this monograph.[1] It is the mandate of the working group to review and assess a range of possible scenarios that contain significant potential for strategic surprise and unanticipated outcomes relating to U.S. foreign policy. As such, the second half of the April 26, 2004, meeting focused on potential surprises that might arise out of the recent use of U.S. power. Limited in time and scope, this meeting served as a sounding board for earlier versions of the papers in this monograph. The ideas that follow may offer valuable insights for forecasting, and consequently preparing for, the multiple scenarios that could feasibly result from the current strategic situation.

The Middle East

Paralleling the progression of the monograph, the discussion of possible surprises first turned to events that might flow from U.S. policies

---

[1]The Schlesinger Working Group relies on a permanent "core membership" of generalists from policymaking and research communities and academia, who are joined by some half-dozen respected authorities recruited for the regional or functional topic under consideration. The working group falls under co-chairs Chester A. Crocker, Schlesinger professor of strategic studies and ISD board member, and Casimir A. Yost, ISD director.

in the Middle East and Iraq. Participants began by acknowledging that so much of contemporary analysis predicts negative outcomes that true surprises would have to be positive ones. To illustrate, no participants predicted a successful outcome in Iraq, short of pulling out to prevent further U.S. military over-stretch and casualties.

That said, the possibility of success in some form in Iraq cannot be excluded, and it would certainly surprise many people. Participants did mention the possibility for a multinational force to take charge, either NATO or a UN-led contingent, that might increase the prospects for stability and help to mend strained relations with allies. Participants also observed that significant movement forward in the Israeli-Palestinian peace process would certainly improve the U.S. position in the Middle East and perhaps go a long way in tempering growing opposition in the area, including in Iraq. This was, however, accompanied by a warning that such progress could come at price; for example, the United States could end up with "ownership" of Gaza, which would be yet another factor straining U.S. diplomatic and military efforts.

These few positive surprise scenarios were overwhelmed by a list of possible negative outcomes. Participants mentioned three potential fates for Iraq: (a) a Haiti that might survive for a time and then unravel; (b) a Lebanon, where independence and foreign troop withdrawal is followed by civil war and military intervention by interested neighbors; or (c) a Somalia, where the United Nations would step in and the United States would then blame it for the inevitable failure. Many viewed the consequences of the second option as the most grave. In addition to the complications of attracting neighbors with differing agendas, a Kurdish move toward independence would likely draw in Turkey, thus imperiling internal NATO cohesion.

Each potential scenario for Iraq could also be influenced by other, exogenous situations. Saudi Arabia's secular regime has appeared increasingly vulnerable to domestic unrest, making it ripe for a stumble or worse. The United States has largely left the handling of Iran's not-so-covert nuclear ambitions to its European allies, but Iran might yet take advantage of U.S. neglect to further scuttle negotiations and hasten its race for nuclear weapons. Iran could be expected to play on the notion that the United States needs its assistance, at least tacitly.

Europe

While the general assessment of current U.S.-European relations was fairly grim, participants noted a number of positive scenarios that could improve the transatlantic relationship. One possibility centered on a reinvigorated NATO. A renewed focus on NATO might include the creation of a rapid response force to play an expanding role in peacekeeping and stabilization operations outside the NATO area. Alternatively (or coincidentally), one might see the emergence of enhanced EU capabilities in this field. Such a situation would provide the U.S.'s European allies with a greater voice, more autonomy, and potentially an enhanced readiness to assume a greater international role for itself. (This, of course, would depend critically on European willingness to make necessary investments in defense capacity.) A second possibility would be a combined European-U.S. effort to resuscitate the Israeli-Palestinian peace process, which, if successful, would improve relations both across the Atlantic and in the Middle East.

At the least, many participants believed that the Europeans will act as a safety net. Whatever Europeans thought of the Iraq mission, a complete U.S. failure would hardly be tolerable. Eventually, some argued, the allies would step in and attempt to make the best of things. The question would be how and when Europe perceives a looming failure worthy of rescue and whether this threshold is shared by all states. In the end, such a positive surprise dynamic will depend substantially on a parallel recognition on both sides of the Atlantic that a permanent rift or decisive rupture are unacceptable.

Besides these possible upswings in relations, some participants did envision scenarios that would not benefit U.S. interests in Europe. Some wondered if the decreasing U.S. military presence and political capital might allow problems to fester in Eastern Europe. The declining U.S. presence may not adequately discourage growing Russian interests in the near-abroad. It also decreases the focus on the still unsettled Balkans region. Ultimately, the use of U.S. power in the Middle East may lead to errors of omission in parts of Europe.

Asia

Participants pegged possible surprises in Asia as stemming more from strategic indifference (both from the U.S. and Asian states) rather than direct reaction to U.S. policies. The United States has enjoyed direct support or benign indifference from a number of states that might otherwise seem opposed to the use of U.S. power, most notably China and India. Participants speculated that China could continue to allow the United States to marginalize itself in Asia, as demonstrated by its deteriorating relations with South Korea. This would enable China to exploit the growing political vacuum for its own purposes, and perhaps most importantly, to shore up its economic and political power in the region. (China's role in the North Korean nuclear crisis might be indicative of this trend.) The United States may not be in a position to vehemently oppose this strategic realignment, and at some point the United States may no longer have an indispensable role in Asia. On the other hand, however, other participants were quick to warn that such a scenario could face many obstacles. First, a Chinese economic bust would dampen this possibility and leave the region with an unanticipated political vacuum. Second, it is not clear whether the level of U.S. indifference or distraction required for this to occur has been or will be reached.

Other surprises might come from South Asia. If Pakistan's Musharraf were to lose power, one participant noted that this would not necessarily engender doom. Rather, Musharraf would most likely be replaced by a similar military dictator or a weak civilian government strongly influenced by the military. This scenario did not project complications for the war on terrorism, either from Pakistan or through Afghanistan. The surprise in South Asia, in sum, could be that the worst case of state failure in Pakistan and the loss of this ally in the war on terrorism *does not* occur.

The Implications for U.S. Grand Strategy

The working group also identified broader, strategic implications for the use of U.S. power. Militarily, participants issued stark warnings about the readiness and strength of the U.S. military. Deployments to

Afghanistan and Iraq have already stretched the military, and particularly the army, thinly, arguably putting it near the threshold of "breaking," potentially imperiling both of these operations and the war on terrorism. The effects could be international in the form of conflict or outright civil war in Iraq, or domestic in the form of ballooning budget deficits and politically unpopular decisions to bolster military capacity.

An excessive U.S. focus on the Middle East could allow for distractions beyond Europe and Asia. One participant stated that Latin American contingencies—such as Castro's long-anticipated fall, strife in Venezuela, or Mexican unrest—could find the Europeans jumping in ahead of the United States to offer an alternative pole of policy initiative. This would only add to the potential loss of U.S. influence that might already be occurring in Europe and Asia. Some wondered if this imbalance in apparent U.S. global interests is desirable or sustainable.

Although the possibility of negative outcomes dominated discussion, potential opportunities for improvement were not overlooked. Some predicted that the United States might have some major successes in the war on terrorism, whether it is the capture of a key figure or the successful defeat of terrorism in a vulnerable state or region (such as Africa). Such a success could help rally domestic and international support. On a strategic level, some observed that the United States might become less adventurous after its recent, difficult Iraqi and Afghanistan experiences, which might provide an opportunity for the United States and its allies to readjust and adapt their relations in the wake of an especially unhappy experience of acrimonious divisions.

About the Authors

Stanley R. Sloan

Stanley Sloan is the founding Director of the Atlantic Community Initiative, a Visiting Scholar at the Rohatyn Center for International Affairs at Middlebury College, and President of VIC–Vermont, a private consulting firm. He is associated with the Swiss-based Strategy Consulting Partners and Associates (SCPA) and serves on the Advisory Board of the Düsseldorf Institute for Foreign and Security Policy.

Mr. Sloan was educated at the University of Maine (BA), Columbia's School of International Affairs (MIA), and American University's School of International Service. He is a Distinguished Graduate of the Air Force Officers' Training School and served as a commissioned officer in the U.S. Air Force. Mr. Sloan began his more than three decades of public service at the Central Intelligence Agency in 1967, serving as NATO and European Community desk officer, member of the U.S. Delegation to the Negotiations on Mutual and Balanced Force Reductions, and as Deputy National Intelligence Officer for Western Europe.

Mr. Sloan was employed by the Congressional Research Service in a variety of analytical and managerial positions from 1975 to 1999. In April 1999, he retired from his position as the senior specialist in International Security Policy. During 1997–98, he was the rapporteur for the North Atlantic Assembly's special presidential report on "NATO in the 21st Century." From 1997 to 1999, he was the adviser to the Senate NATO Observer Group.

Mr. Sloan's recent books and monographs include *NATO, the European Union and the Atlantic Community: The Transatlantic Bargain Reconsidered* (Rowman and Littlefield, November 2002); *NATO and Transatlantic Relations in the 21st Century: Crisis,*

Continuity or Change? (Foreign Policy Association, October 2002); *The United States and European Defence* (Chaillot Paper, Western European Union Institute, April 2000); *The Foreign Policy Struggle— Congress and the President in the 1990s and Beyond* [with Mary Locke and Casimir A. Yost] (Georgetown University Institute for the Study of Diplomacy, January 2000).

Robert G. Sutter

Robert Sutter has been a visiting professor in the School of Foreign Service at Georgetown University since August 2001.

Dr. Sutter specialized in Asian and Pacific Affairs and U.S. foreign policy in a U.S. government career of thirty years. He held a variety of analytical and supervisory positions with the Library of Congress for more than twenty years, and he also worked with the Central Intelligence Agency, the Department of State, and the Senate Foreign Relations Committee. After leaving the Library of Congress, where he was for many years the senior specialist in international politics for the Congressional Research Service, Dr. Sutter served for two years as the National Intelligence Officer for East Asia and the Pacific at the U.S. government's National Intelligence Council.

He received a Ph.D. in History and East Asian Languages from Harvard University. He has held adjunct faculty positions with Georgetown, George Washington, and the Johns Hopkins Universities and the University of Virginia. He has published thirteen books, numerous articles, and several hundred government reports dealing with contemporary East Asian and Pacific countries and their relations with the United States. His most recent book is *The United States and East Asia: Dynamics and Implications* (Rowman and Littlefield, 2003).

Casimir A. Yost

Casimir A. Yost is the director of the Institute for the Study of Diplomacy (ISD) and Marshall B. Coyne Professor in the Practice of Diplomacy in the Edmund A. Walsh School of Foreign Service at Georgetown University.

Professor Yost served, before coming to Georgetown University, as executive director of the Asia Foundation's Center for Asian Pacific Affairs (CAPA) in San Francisco. Prior to that, he was president of the World Affairs Council of Northern California. From 1982 to 1986, he served on the professional staff of the Committee on Foreign Relations of the U.S. Senate under Senator Charles Percy and Senator Richard Lugar. From 1977 to 1982, Professor Yost was foreign policy adviser to Senator Charles McC. Mathias, Jr. (R-Md.). Between 1972 and 1977, he worked for Citibank of New York in Lebanon, Pakistan, Saudi Arabia, and Tunisia.

Professor Yost co-chairs ISD's Schlesinger Working Group on Strategic Surprises and the annual meetings of the International Forum on Diplomatic Training. Professor Yost also consults with the U.S. government.

He is a graduate of Hamilton College with a B.A. in History and has a Master's of Science in Foreign Service degree from Georgetown University. He is a member of the Council on Foreign Relations and the National Committee on United States-China Relations. He is a member of the Board of Trustees of the Asia Foundation.